Strands
OF COLOR

- BY KNIT PICKS -

Copyright 2017 © Knit Picks

All rights reserved. This book or any portion thereof may not be reproduced or used in any manner whatsoever without the express written permission of the publisher except for the use of brief quotations in a book review.

Photography by Amy Cave

Printed in the United States of America

First Printing, 2017

ISBN 978-1-62767-170-5

Versa Press, Inc
800-447-7829

www.versapress.com

CONTENTS

Arrows Headband	4
Classical Snow Mittens	8
Vesterland Hat	12
Rafinesque Cowl	16
Snowtime Beanie	20
Allover Patterned Scarf	24
Little Orme	28
Morgan Mitts	32
Fireside Tablet Cover	42
Shea Cowl	46
Snow Day Tea Cozy	50
To The Top Hat	54
Blodwen Cowl	58
Hot Water Bottle Cover	62
Shaela Cowl	66

ARROWS HEADBAND

by Abbyeknits

FINISHED MEASUREMENTS
19.5 (20.5, 21.5, 22.25)" long x 4" wide; garment is meant to be worn with negative 2" ease

YARN
Knit Picks Swish DK (100% Superwash Merino Wool; 123 yards/50g): MC Dove Heather 24956, C1 Hollyberry 24063, C2 Wonderland Heather 26062, C3 Allspice 25579

NEEDLES
US 6 (4mm) straight or circular needles, or size to obtain gauge

NOTIONS
Yarn Needle
Stitch Markers
Tapestry Needle
0.5-1" Button (1)

GAUGE
21 sts and 24 rows = 4" in stranded St st, blocked

Arrows Head Headband

Notes:
This headband is worked flat, and features increases and decreases done on both ends. It has a garter stitch border and stranded stockinette through the main part of the headband. A buttonhole is worked in one end to close the headband.

Read the Chart from bottom to top, RS rows (odd numbers) from right to left, and WS rows (even numbers) from left to right.

DIRECTIONS

Border
With MC, CO 80 (84, 90, 94) sts.

Row 1 (RS): K.
Row 2-5: K1, KFB, K to last 2 sts, KFB, K1. 2 sts inc. 88 (92, 98, 102) sts.

Body
Row 6 (WS): K1, KFB, K2, P0 (2, 0, 2), begin working Chart, P0 (2, 0, 2), K2, KFB, K1. 2 sts inc.

Switch to C3.

Row 7 (RS): K1, KFB, K3 (5, 3, 5), work Chart, K3 (5, 3, 5), KFB, K1. 2 sts inc.
Row 8: K1, KFB, K2, P2 (4, 2, 4), work Chart, P2 (4, 2, 4), K2, KFB, K1. 2 sts inc.
Row 9: K1, KFB, K5 (7, 5, 7), work Chart, K5 (7, 5, 7), KFB, K1. 2 sts inc.
Row 10: K1, KFB, K2, P4 (6, 4, 6), work Chart, P4 (6, 4, 6), K2, KFB, K1. 2 sts inc.

Switch to MC.

Row 11: K1, KFB, K7 (9, 7, 9), work Chart, K7 (9, 7, 9), KFB, K1. 2 sts inc.
Row 12: K1, KFB, K2, P6 (8, 6, 8), work Chart, P6 (8, 6, 8), K2, KFB, K1. 2 sts inc.
Row 13: K11 (13, 11, 13), work Chart, K6 (8, 6, 8), BO 3, K2.
Row 14: K2, CO 2 sts, P6 (8, 6, 8), work Chart, P6 (8, 6, 8), K2, K2tog, K1. 10 (104, 110, 114) sts.
Row 15: K1, K2tog, K7 (9, 7, 9), work Chart, K7 (9, 7, 9), K2tog, K1. 2 sts dec.

Switch to C3.

Row 16: K1, K2tog, K2, P4 (6, 4, 6), work Chart, P4 (6, 4, 6), K2, K2tog, K1. 2 sts dec.
Row 17: K1, K2tog, K5 (7, 5, 7), work Chart, K5 (7, 5, 7), K2tog, K1. 2 sts dec.
Row 18: K1, K2tog, K2, P2 (4, 2, 4), work Chart, P2 (4, 2, 4), K2, K2tog, K1. 2 sts dec.
Row 19: K1, K2tog, K3 (5, 3, 5), work Chart, K3 (5, 3, 5), K2tog, K1. 2 sts dec.

Switch to MC.

Row 20: K1, K2tog, K2, P0 (2, 0, 2), work Chart, P2, P0 (2, 0, 2), K2tog, K1. 2 sts dec.

Border
Row 21-24: K1, K2tog, K to last 3 sts, K2tog, K1. 2 sts dec.
Row 25: K.

BO all sts.

Finishing
Weave in ends, wash and block to finished measurements. Sew button onto end opposite of button hole.

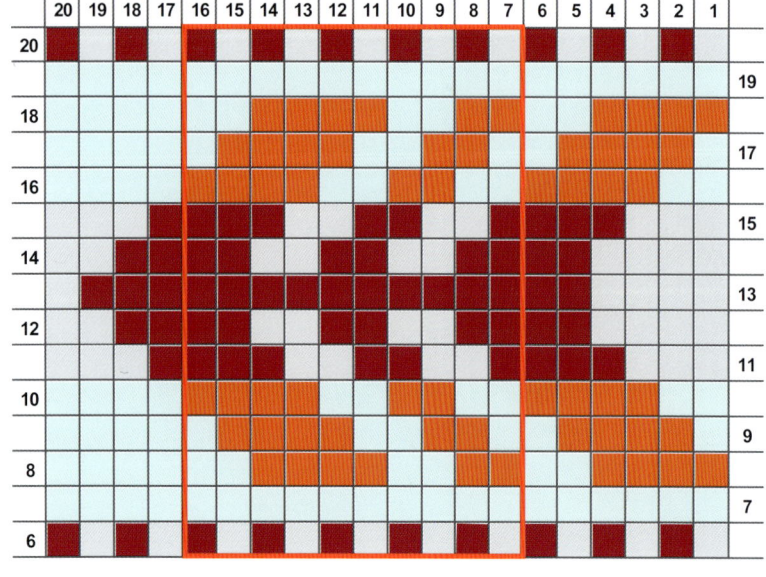

Arrows Head Headband Chart

Legend:

 Knit
RS: knit stitch
WS: purl stitch

 MC

C1

C2

 C3

 Pattern Repeat

CLASSICAL SNOW MITTENS

by Erica Jackofsky

FINISHED MEASUREMENTS
8" palm circumference x 7.25" length from wrist to fingertips (excluding ribbing), length after thumb can be adjusted

YARN
Knit Picks Wool of the Andes Sport (100% Peruvian Highland Wool; 137 yards/50g): C1 Mink Heather 25275, C2 Fedora 25272, C3 Bramble Heather 25278, C4 Hollyberry 25298, 1 ball each

NEEDLES
US 5 (3.75mm) DPNs or two 24" circular needles for two circulars technique, or one 32" or longer circular needle for Magic Loop technique, or size to obtain gauge
US 3 (3.25mm) DPNs or two 24" circular needles for two circulars technique, or one 32" or longer circular needle for Magic Loop technique, or 2 sizes smaller than size to obtain gauge

NOTIONS
Yarn Needle
Stitch Markers
Waste yarn for thumb stitches

GAUGE
24 sts and 30 rnds = 4" in stranded St st in the rnd on larger needles, blocked

For pattern support, contact erica@fiddleknits.com

Classical Snow Mittens

Notes:
You will be casting on with C3 and then immediately cutting that yarn. This will give one thin stripe of the color at the wrist. The next round is worked with C4 and then this yarn is also cut providing a second thin stripe before beginning the 1x1 Rib cuff.

Work the chart from right to left, reading every row as a RS row. The thumb stitches are outlined in the pattern in pink for the Right Mitten and green for the Left Mitten.

1x1 Rib (in the rnd over an even number of sts)
All Rnds: (K1, P1) to end of rnd.

Kitchener Stitch
Kitchener st is used to create a seamless look in your knitting. Here it is used to finish the top og the mitten.
Step 1: Thread a tapestry needle with the long tail at the end of your knitting, or use another length of matching yarn.
Step 2: Divide your sts evenly between 2 needles and hold needles parallel to each other. Make sure the RS of the fabric faces out and both needle tips point in the same direction.
Step 3: Insert tapestry needle into the first st on the front needle as if to P. Pull yarn through leaving the st on needle.
Step 4: Insert tapestry needle into the first st on the back needle as if to K. Pull yarn through leaving the st on needle.
Step 5: Insert tapestry needle into the first st on the front needle as if to K. Pull yarn through and Sl st from needle.
Step 6: Insert tapestry needle in next st on the front needle as if to P. Pull yarn through and leave the st on needle.
Step 7: Insert tapestry needle into the first st on the back needle as if to P. Pull yarn through and Sl st from needle.
Step 8: Insert tapestry needle in next st on the back needle as if to K. Pull yarn through and leave the st on needle.
*Repeat Steps 5 – 8 until all sts have been grafted together. When you have 2 sts left work Step 5 & then Step 7. Fasten off and weave in end.

DIRECTIONS

Cuff
With C3 and smaller needles, CO 48 sts. PM and join for working in the rnd, being careful not to twist sts.
Cut yarn and attach C4.
P 1 rnd
Cut yarn and attach C1
K 1 rnd.
Work 1x1 Rib for 2"
K 1 rnd.

Hand
Change to larger needles and work Rnds 1-19 of the Classical Snow Hand chart.

Left and right mittens are worked the same through Rnd 19.

Thumb Base
Rnd 20, Right Mitten Only: Work in charted pattern across first 27 sts of rnd, K7 with waste yarn. Place these 7 sts back on the left needle and finish working across rnd in charted pattern.

Rnd 20, Left Mitten Only: Work in charted pattern across first 39 sts of rnd, K7 with waste yarn. Place these 7 sts back on the left needle and finish working across rnd in charted pattern.

Hand, Continued
Complete Hand by working Rnds 21-54 of the Classical Snow Hand Chart.

Rnds 34-37 can be repeated to add additional length before beginning decreases on the mitten top. Each extra repeat will add approximately 0.5" additional length.

Place 8 sts from top of hand on one needle and 8 sts from palm on a second needle and hold parallel to each other. Use C3 and Kitchener st the mitten top closed.

Thumb
Carefully remove waste yarn at thumb.

Divide 7 lower sts and 7 upper sts onto needles.

Rnd 1: With C2, PU & K1 st at edge of thumb, K7, PM, PU & K1 st, K7, PM and join for working in the rnd. 16 sts.

Knit even for 2.5", or until thumb is desired length.

Dec Rnd 1: (K1, SSK, K3, K2tog) twice. 12 sts.
Dec Rnd 2: (K1, SSK, K1, K2tog) twice. 8 sts.
Last Rnd: (K1, SKP, K1) twice. 6 sts.

Cut yarn and thread tail of C2 through remaining sts, and fasten off.

Repeat for second mitten.

Finishing
Weave in ends, wash and block. Do not block ribbed cuff.

Classical Snow Hand Chart

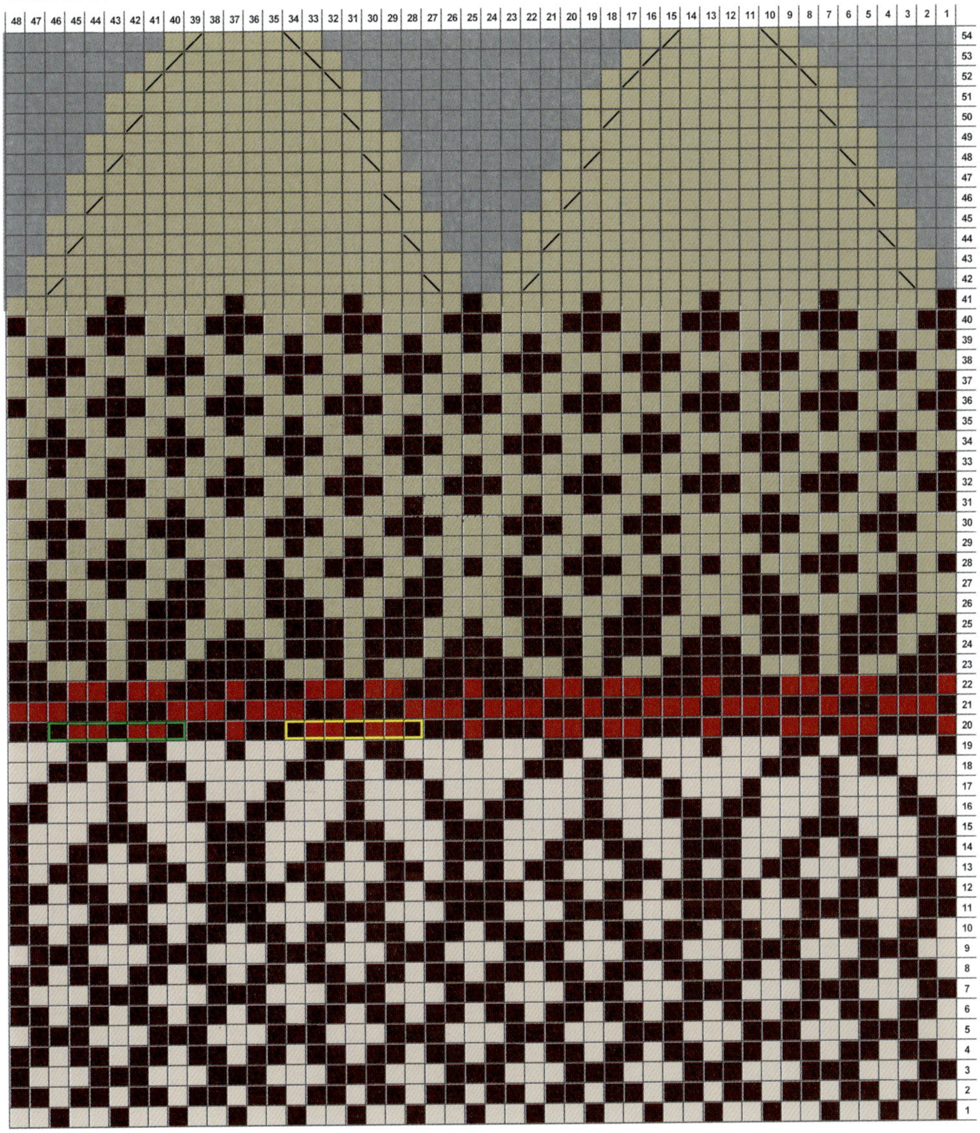

Legend:

- ☐ **knit** — Knit stitch
- ■ **No Stitch** — Placeholder - No stitch made.
- ⧅ **ssk** — Slip one stitch as if to knit, Slip another stitch as if to knit. Insert left-hand needle into front of these 2 stitches and knit them together
- ⧄ **k2tog** — Knit two stitches together as one stitch
- ▨ C1
- ■ C2
- ▨ C3
- ■ C4
- ▭ Right Thumb stitches
- ▭ Left Thumb stitches

Classical Snow Mittens

VESTERLAND HAT

by Bridget Pupillo

FINISHED MEASUREMENTS
17.25 (20, 22.75)" circumference x 7.25 (8, 8.75)" tall, to fit 17-19 (20-22, 23-24)" head circumference

YARN
Knit Picks Palette (100% Peruvian Highland Wool; 231 yards/50g):
MC Calypso Heather 24009, C1 Midnight Heather 25540, C2 Cream 23730, C3 Pimento 24246, 1 ball each

NEEDLES
US 4 (3.5mm) 16" circular needles and DPNs or two 24" circular needles for two circulars technique, or one 32" or longer circular needle for Magic Loop technique, or size to obtain gauge
US 3 (3.25mm) 16" circular needles, or one size smaller than size to obtain gauge

NOTIONS
Stitch Marker
Large Yarn Needle

GAUGE
28 sts and 34 rnds = 4" in stranded St st in the rnd on larger needles, blocked.

Vesterland Hat

Notes:

The Vesterland Hat is knitted in the round from the bottom up, beginning with the band lining. The band and crown are worked using Stranded Knitting technique, with standard decreases to shape the crown. The band lining is folded and sewn under, and the hat is topped with an optional braided tassel.

All charts are worked in stranded St st in the round, with all chart rows being read from right to left as RS rows.Re

Stranded Knitting tutorial can be found at http://tutorials.knitpicks.com/fair-isle-or-stranded-knitting/.

Stockinette Stitch (St st, worked in the round over any number of sts)
Rnd 1 (RS): Knit
Rep rnd 1 for pattern.

Reverse Stockinette Stitch (rev st st, worked in the round over any number of sts)
Rnd 1 (RS): Purl
Rep rnd 1 for pattern.

DIRECTIONS

Body

With smaller needles and MC, CO 120 (140, 160) sts. PM and join to work in the rnd, being careful not to twist sts.
Work in St st for 25 rnds.
Continuing in St st, join C1 and work one rnd.
Work two rnds in MC.
Continuing in MC, work one rnd in rev St st.
Switch to larger size needles. Work Band Chart, repeating Band Chart sts 6 (7, 8) times around.
Break C1. Continuing in MC, work one more rnd in St st and two more rnds in rev St st. Break MC.

Crown

Join C2 and C3 and work to Rnd 14 of Crown Chart, repeating Crown Chart sts 6 (7, 8) times around.
17.25" Size: Continue to last rnd of Crown Chart.
20" Size: Rep Rnds 9-14 of Crown Chart once more, then continue to last rnd of Crown Chart.
22.75" Size: Rep Rnds 9-14 of Crown Chart twice more, then continue to last rnd of Crown Chart.

All Sizes: Break C3 and continue with C2.
Next Two Rnds: K2tog around. 6 (7, 8) sts remain.
Break C2, thread yarn tail through remaining sts two times. Pull snug and pull yarn tail through to WS.

Finishing

Weave in ends.

Fold band lining under at first rev St st rnd and sew hem loosely to inside of hat.

Wash and block to measurements.

Optional Tassel

Cut four 36" lengths of MC and eight 36" lengths of C1.

Knot all strands together, leaving a tail approximately 3" in length. Thread the longer ends of all strands through a large yarn needle and pull through the center of the hat's crown from WS to RS. Pull until the knot is snug against the inside of the hat. Separate into three equal sections of 4 strands each. Make a tight braid 3" in length.

Knot all strands together at the end of the braid, leaving the knot very loose (see Figure 1). Thread the ends of all the strands through the knot just made, so that the strands make a loop approximately 12" around, and the loose ends hang down approximately 6" in length (see Figure 2). Pull the knot tight (Figure 3).

Thread one of the loose ends of C1 through yarn needle. Hold all strands together tightly. Wrap the strand of C1 around the bundle three times. Pull needle through center of tassel and pull snug. This will form the tassel.

Trim tassel ends to desired length. Trim tail inside the hat to .5" in length.

Vesterland Hat Crown Chart

Vesterland Hat Band Chart

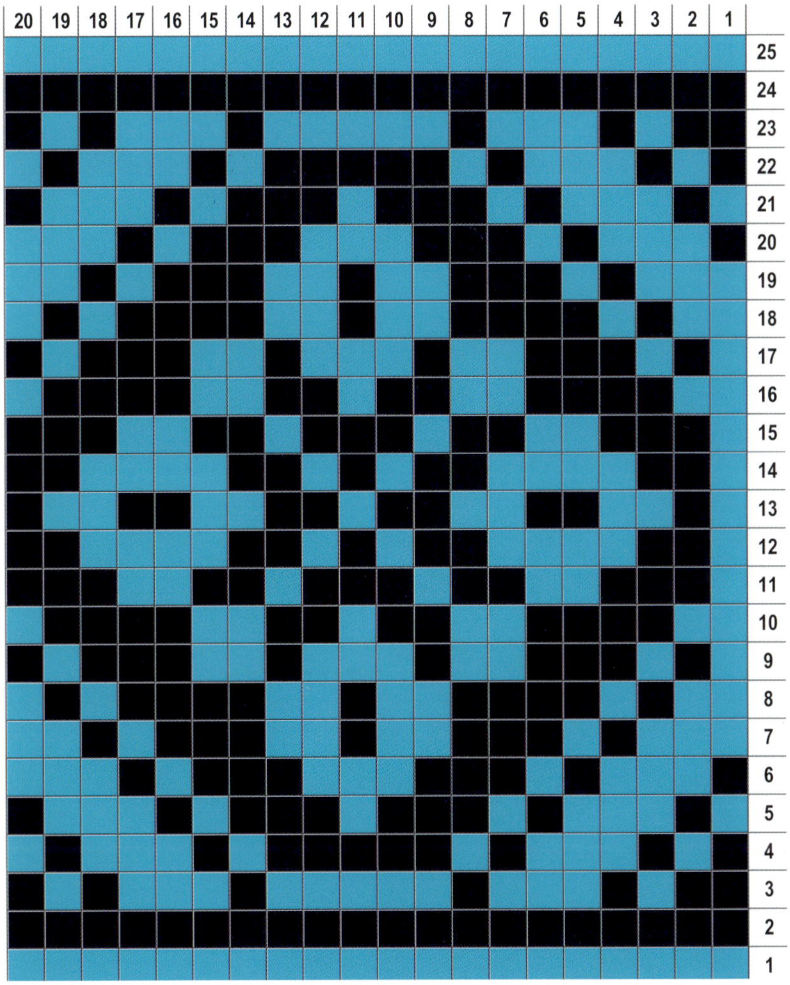

20 19 18 17 16 15 14 13 12 11 10 9 8 7 6 5 4 3 2 1
25 24 23 22 21 20 19 18 17 16 15 14 13 12 11 10 9 8 7 6 5 4 3 2 1

Legend:

- **knit** – knit stitch
- **no stitch** – Placeholder - No stitch made.
- **k2tog** – Knit two stitches together as one stitch
- **ssk** – Slip one stitch as if to knit, Slip another stitch as if to knit. Insert left-hand needle into front of these 2 stitches and knit them together
- repeat
- MC
- C1
- C2
- C3

Tassel Instructions

1

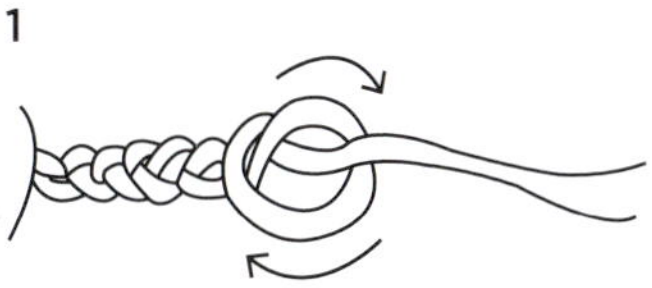

2

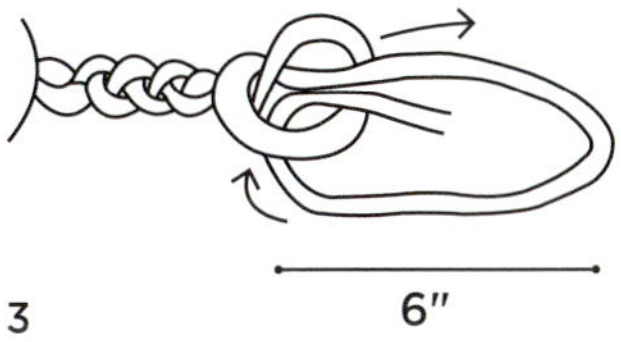
6″

3

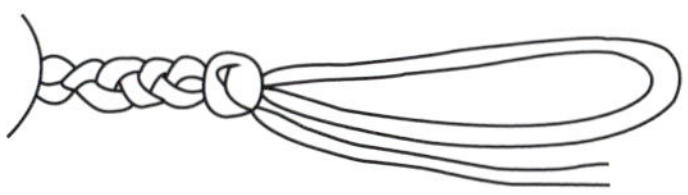

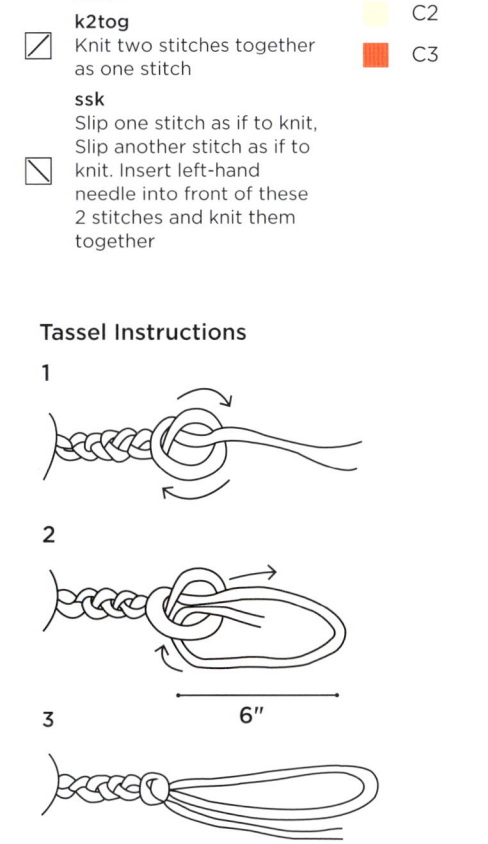

RAFINESQUE COWL

by Zabet Kempfert

FINISHED MEASUREMENTS
9.5" tall x 31" circumference, blocked

YARN
Knit Picks Swish Worsted (100% Superwash Merino Wool; 110 yards/50g): MC Wonderland Heather 26067, 2 balls; C1 Cobblestone Heather 24661, 2 balls; C2 White 24662, 2 balls; C3 Dove Heather 25631, 1 ball; C4 Hollyberry 25148, 2 balls

NEEDLES
US 7 (4.5mm) DPNs or circular needles, or size to obtain gauge

NOTIONS
Yarn Needle
Stitch Markers
Scrap yarn for Provisional CO
Spare Circular Needle

GAUGE
21 sts and 24 rnds = 4" in stranded St st in the rnd, blocked

Rafinesque Cowl

Notes:

The Rafinesque Cowl is worked in the round as a long tube, beginning with a provisional cast on. After knitting the stranded body of the tube, the two ends are grafted together to form a seamless, double-layered cowl. Two sets of slipped stitches are worked every other row alongside the main Fair Isle pattern, in order to make the cowl lie flat and not twist on itself.

If you wish to make a longer cowl, simply increase the number of chart repeats that you knit. Remember to end the final repeat on Row 61 of the Rafinesque Chart.

While the majority of the piece is knit in traditional two-color Fair Isle, Rnds 42-46 and 48-52 are knit with three colors in each round. Feel free to work the C4 stitches in those rounds with C1 to make the stranding easier.

Because the cowl is worked in the round, there is no need to weave in your ends. However, make sure to secure each end as you go so that they do not become loose.

DIRECTIONS
Cowl

Using the Provisional CO of your choice, CO 100 sts. With MC, K 1 row and join to work in the round, being careful not to twist sts. PM at beginning of the rnd and after 50 sts.

Join C1 and C2 and begin working from Rafinesque Chart, starting with Row 2. Work the 50 st pattern 2 times around the cowl, reading each chart row from right to left. Work Rnds 2-62 once.

Work Rnds 1-62 once.

Work Rnds 1-61 once.

Break all yarns leaving a 2 yard tail of MC. Place provisionally CO sts onto spare set of needles. Using MC, graft beginning and end together, making sure to match up beginning of rnds.

Finishing

Weave in MC end, wash, and block to finished measurements.

Rafinesque Chart

Legend
- ☐ **knit** knit stitch
- V slip stitch
- ■ MC
- ■ C1
- ☐ C2
- ■ C3
- ■ C4

Rafinesque Cowl 19

SNOWTIME BEANIE

by Erica Jackofsky

FINISHED MEASUREMENTS
19.25" circumference, relaxed

YARN
Knit Picks Palette (100% Peruvian Highland Wool; 231 yards/50g): MC Asphalt 24243, C1 Oyster Heather 24559, C2 Clarity 25548, C3 Hollyberry 25539, 1 ball each

NEEDLES
US 1.5 (2.5mm) 16" circular needles, or 2 sizes smaller than size to obtain gauge

US 3 (3.25mm) 16" circular needles, and DPNs or two circular needles, or size to obtain gauge

NOTIONS
Yarn Needle
Stitch Markers

GAUGE
30 sts and 32 rnds = 4" in stranded St st in the rnd on larger needles, blocked

Snowtime Beanie

Notes:
The Snowtime Beanie is worked from the ribbing up through the crown decreases. No round will use more than 2 colors at a time. Work the chart from right to left, reading every row as a RS row.

DIRECTIONS
Brim
With smaller needles and C3, CO 144 sts.
PM and join for working in the rnd, being careful not to twist sts.
Cut C3 and attach MC
K 1 rnd.

Rnd 1: *K1, P2, K1; rep from * to end of rnd.
Rep Rnd 1 for 1.5"

Change to larger needles.

Hat
Work Rnds 1-55 of the Snowtime Beanie chart (includes decrease section), working chart 4 times around.
Cut yarn and pull tail through remaining 8 sts.

Finishing
Weave in ends and block upper portion of hat as desired. Do not block ribbing.

Snowtime Beanie Chart

Legend:
- knit — Knit stitch
- No Stitch — Placeholder - No stitch made.
- ssk — Slip one stitch as if to knit, Slip another stitch as if to knit. Insert left-hand needle into front of these 2 stitches and knit them together
- k2tog — Knit two stitches together as one stitch
- MC
- C1
- C2
- C3

ALLOVER PATTERNED SCARF

by Faye Kennington

FINISHED MEASUREMENTS
5.75" wide at widest point x 64.5" long, including 3" pom-poms on each end

YARN
Knit Picks Swish DK (100% Superwash Merino Wool; 123 yards/50g): MC Lava Heather 25584, 2 balls; C1 Garnet Heather 24315, 1 ball; C2 Delft Heather 24312, 1 ball; C3 White 24064, 2 balls; C4 Rainforest Heather 25585, 1 ball; C5 Wonderland Heather 26062, 2 balls

NEEDLES
US 5 (3.75mm) DPNs or two 24" circular needles for two circulars technique, or one 32" or longer circular needle for Magic Loop technique, or one size smaller than size to obtain gauge
US 6 (4mm) DPNs or two 24" circular needles for two circulars technique, or one 32" or longer circular needle for Magic Loop technique, or size to obtain gauge

NOTIONS
Yarn Needle
Stitch Marker
3 3/8" Pom-pom Maker (optional)
Crochet Hook

GAUGE
23 sts and 25 rows = 4" in stranded St st in the rnd with larger needles, blocked

For pattern support, contact faye@coastandtoast.com

Allover Patterned Scarf

Notes:
This pattern is knit in a tube with increases and decreases on each end that come to tips and are trimmed with pom-poms. A stranded colorwork chart is repeated six times in the round to make the bulk of the scarf.

Smaller needles are suggested for the non-stranded sections on each end as stranded knitting tends to be a bit tighter than St st. Use whatever size needle will achieve the same stitch gauge for the St st sections.

Because the yarn ends are encased in the finished scarf, there is no need to weave in the ends. As you work, adjust any stitches that appear loose on the right side by gently pulling any excess yarn to the wrong side. Yarns do not have to be cut at the end of a round if they will be used again in the next 6-10 rounds; just take care to watch the tension on the wrong side.

Emily Ocker's Circular Cast-On Method
Make a loop of yarn about 4.5" in circumference with the yarn tail hanging down. With a crochet hook, *pull a st through main loop, then draw a third st through the second st. Rep from * for each st to be cast on. Transfer sts to DPNs or desired needles. After several rnds have been worked, pull on the yarn tail to tighten the initial loop and close the circle.

When working the chart in the rnd, follow all chart rows from right to left, reading them as RS rows.

DIRECTIONS

Scarf

Increases
With MC and crochet hook, using Emily Ocker's Circular Cast-on Method, CO 6 sts. Arrange sts on smaller needles to begin working in the rnd, being careful not to twist sts.

Rnd 1 and all odd rnds through Rnd 19: K to end.
Rnd 2: (K1, M1) to end. 12 sts.
Rnd 4: (K2, M1) to end. 18 sts.
Rnd 6: (K3, M1) to end. 24 sts.
Rnd 8: (K4, M1) to end. 30 sts.
Rnd 10: (K5, M1) to end. 36 sts.
Rnd 12: (K6, M1) to end. 42 sts.
Rnd 14: (K7, M1) to end. 48 sts.
Rnd 16: (K8, M1) to end. 54 sts.
Rnd 18: (K9, M1) to end. 60 sts.
Rnd 20: (K10, M1) to end. 66 sts.
Rnds 21 & 22: K to end.

Colorwork
Using larger needles, work Allover Patterned Scarf Chart Rows 1-54, repeating the 6 sts of each rnd 11 times. Work Chart Rnds 1-54 five more times.

If desired, look over the work and make any necessary tension adjustments. After this point, it will be more difficult to pull excess yarns from loosened sts to the WS. Weave in ends if desired.

Decreases
Using MC and smaller needles, return to St st and dec to 6 sts.

Rnds 1, 2 & 3: K to end.
Rnd 4: (K9, K2tog) to end. 60 sts.
Rnd 6: (K8, K2tog) to end. 54 sts.
Rnd 8: (K7, K2tog) to end. 48 sts.
Rnd 10: (K6, K2tog) to end. 42 sts.
Rnd 12: (K5, K2tog) to end. 36 sts.
Rnd 14: (K4, K2tog) to end. 30 sts.
Rnd 16: (K3, K2tog) to end. 24 sts.
Rnd 18: (K2, K2tog) to end. 18 sts.
Rnd 20: (K1, K2tog) to end. 12 sts.
Rnd 22: (K2tog) to end. 6 sts.

Cut yarn leaving an 8" tail. Pull yarn tail through remaining sts, cinch and secure to close.

Finishing
Weave in ends and block lightly with steam iron. Make 2 pom-poms with MC and attach one to each end at point.

Allover Patterned Scarf

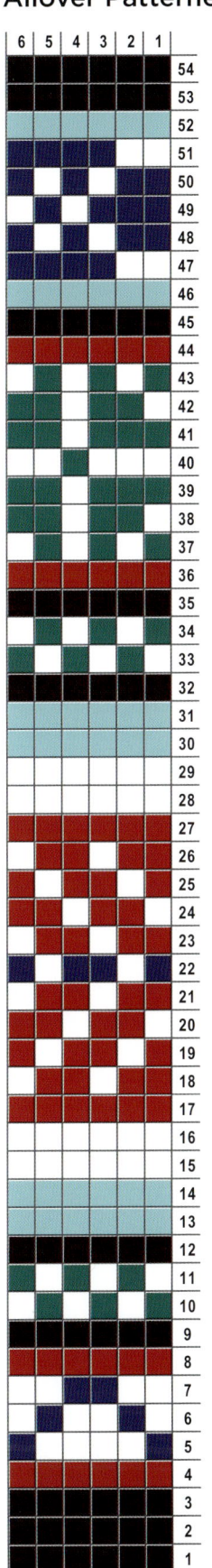

Legend:
- ☐ knit / knit stitch
- ■ MC
- ■ C1
- ■ C2
- ☐ C3
- ■ C4
- ■ C5

LITTLE ORME

by Kath Andrews

FINISHED MEASUREMENTS
7 (7.5, 8)" palm circumference x 7.5 (7.75, 8)" long; mitts are meant to be worn with slight negative ease

YARN
Knit Picks Palette (100% Peruvian Highland Wool; 231 yards/50g): MC Mist 23733, C1 Forest Heather 24584, C2 Spearmint 24253, C3 Celadon Heather 24254, 1 ball each

NEEDLES
US 2 (2.75mm) DPNs or two 24" circular needles for two circulars technique, or one 32" or longer circular needle for Magic Loop technique, or one size smaller than size to obtain gauge

US 3 (3.25mm) DPNs or two 24" circular needles for two circulars technique, or one 32" or longer circular needle for Magic Loop technique, or size to obtain gauge

NOTIONS
Yarn Needle
2 Stitch Markers
Scrap yarn

GAUGE
32 sts and 34 rnds = 4" in stranded St st in the rnd on larger needle, blocked

Little Orme

Notes:
Both Mitts are identical as the pattern flows right around the back and front of the hand

Special Increases
The increases used on the thumb allow a clear line of stitches to be established running up the sides of the thumb, by using lifted increases as follows:
Lifted Increase Right (LIR): On the next st to be worked, lift the right leg of the st below that on the left needle onto the needle and knit into it.
Lifted Increase Left (LIL): Lift the left leg of the st below that of the st just worked on the right needle onto the left needle and knit into it.

2x2 Ribbing (worked in the rnd over multiple of 4 sts)
All Rnds: (K2, P2) to end.

Work all charts in the rnd, follow all chart rows from right to left, reading them as RS rows.

DIRECTIONS
Mitts (make 2)
Cuff
Using smaller needles and MC, loosely CO 52 (56, 60) sts and join to work in the round being careful not to twist. PM for start of rnd.

Ribbing
Using MC, work 2x2 Ribbing for 4 (6, 8) rnds.
Join C1 (do not cut MC), work 2x2 Ribbing for 2 rnds. Cut C1.
Using MC, work 2x2 Ribbing for 4 rnds.
Join C2 (do not cut MC), work 2x2 Ribbing for 2 rnds. Cut C2.
Using MC, work 2x2 Ribbing for 4 rnds.
Join C3 (do not cut MC), work 2x2 Ribbing for 2 rnds. Cut C3.
Using MC, work 2x2 Ribbing for 4 rnds.

Body of Mitt
Change to larger needles and begin working Little Orme Main Chart from Rnd 1, starting at column st 5 (3, 1) and working through chart to column st 56 (58, 60), until Rnd 5 is complete.

Begin Thumb Gusset
Rnd 6: The st marked in a red box (column st 5 (3, 1) becomes the first st of the Little Orme Thumb Chart. Work this st, PM, cont Rnd 6 of Main Chart as set to end.

Rnd 7: Using colors as indicated on Little Orme Thumb Chart, LIR, K1, LIL, SM, then, working from column st 6 (4, 2), complete Rnd 7 of Little Orme Main Chart to column st 56 (58, 60).
Cont as set, increasing on Little Orme Thumb Chart as shown to end of Rnd 25. 68 (72, 76) sts.

Remove marker, place 17 thumb sts on scrap yarn and CO 5 sts using Backward Loop method, SM. Remaining marker now marks beginning of rnd. 56, (60, 64) sts.

Rnd 26: Work Little Orme Main Chart from column st 6 (4, 2) to to column st 61 (63, 65), continuing 4-st patt rep through 5 new sts.
Rnds 27-33: Work through remaining rnds of Little Orme Main Chart as set.

Top Cuff Ribbing
Change to smaller needles and using MC, work 2x2 Ribbing for 4 (5, 5) rnds.

Join C1 (do not cut MC), work 2x2 Ribbing for 2 rnds Cut C1.
Using MC, work 2x2 Ribbing for 2 rnds.
BO in patt.

Thumb Cuff Ribbing
Transfer sts on scrap yarn to smaller needles.

Using MC, K17 thumb sts, PU and K1 st before 5 CO sts, PU and K5 sts from the 5 CO sts, PU and K1 st after 5 CO sts, PM. 24 sts. Work 2x2 Ribbing for 2 (3, 4) rnds.

Join C1 (do not cut MC), work 2x2 Ribbing for 2 rnds. Cut C1.
Using MC, work 2x2 Ribbing for 2 rnds.
BO in patt.

Finishing
Wash and block to diagram, leaving ribbing free to pull in. Weave in ends once mitts are dry, taking care to avoid any holes around the thumb cuff where it joins the body of the mitt.

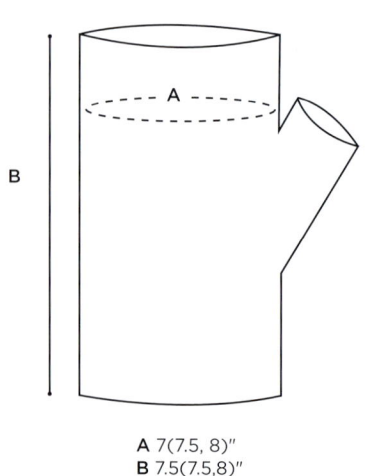

A 7(7.5, 8)"
B 7.5(7.5,8)"

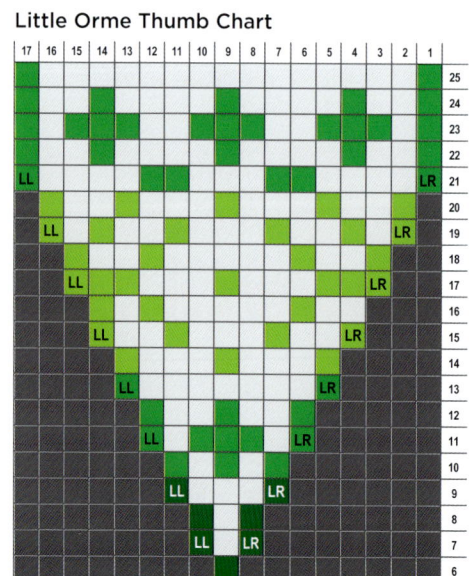

Little Orme Thumb Chart

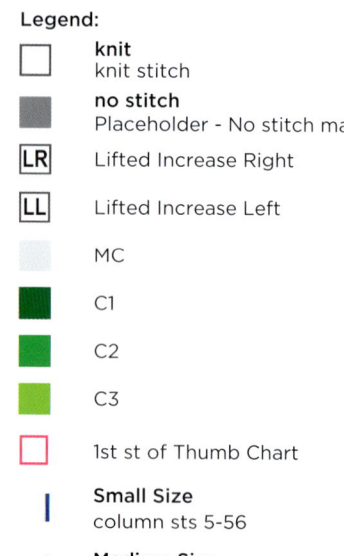

Legend:
- knit — knit stitch
- no stitch — Placeholder - No stitch made
- LR — Lifted Increase Right
- LL — Lifted Increase Left
- MC
- C1
- C2
- C3
- 1st st of Thumb Chart
- **Small Size** column sts 5-56
- **Medium Size** column sts 3-58

Little Orme Main Chart

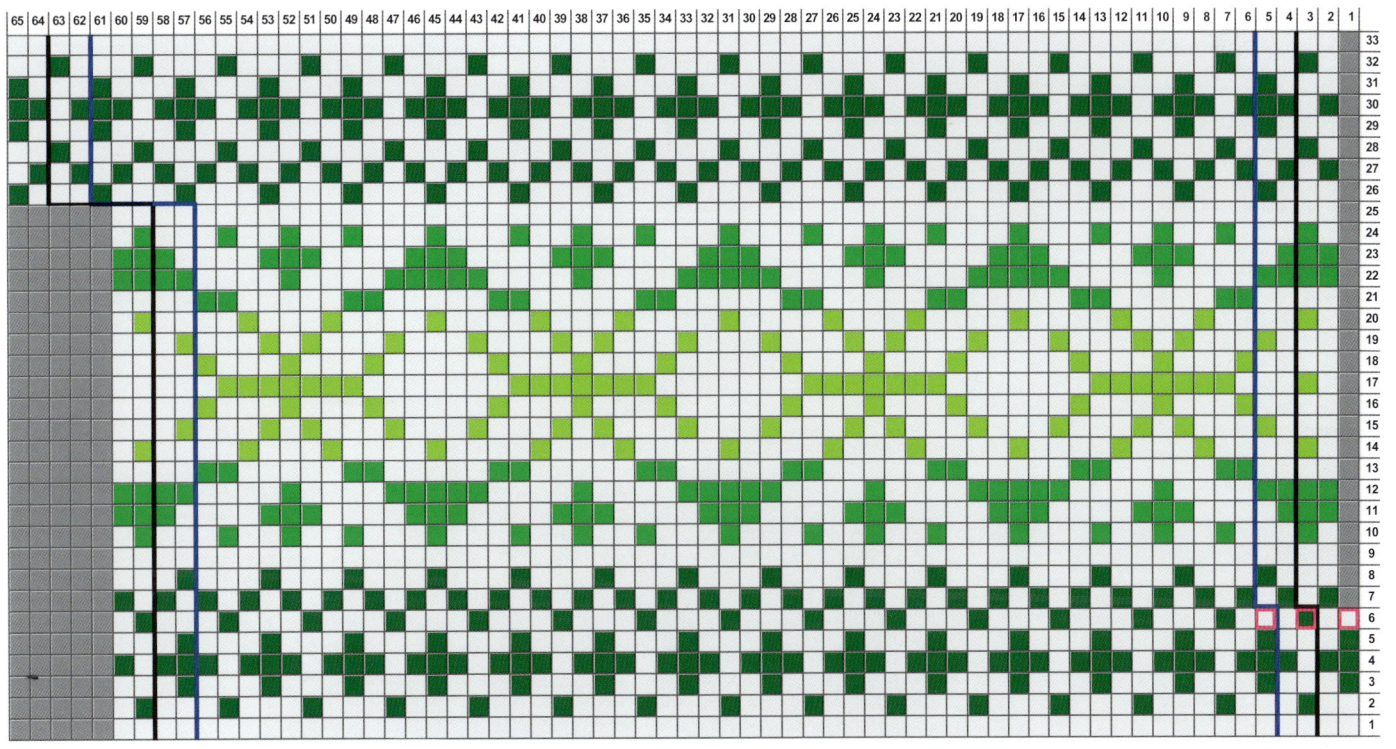

Little Orme 31

MORGAN MITTS

by Stephannie Tallent

FINISHED MEASUREMENTS
6 (7.5, 9)" finished palm circumference

YARN
Knit Picks Palette (100% Peruvian Highland Wool; 231 yards/50g): MC Oyster Heather 24559, C1 Bluebell 24578, C2 Ash 23731, C3 Stellar Heather 26053, C4 Abyss Heather 25993, C5 Serrano 24553, C6 Garnet Heather 24015, C7 Indigo Heather 26051, 1 ball each

NEEDLES
US 2 (3mm) DPNs or two 24" circular needles for two circulars technique, or one 32" or longer circular needle for Magic Loop technique, or size to obtain gauge
US 1 (2.5mm) DPNs or two 24" circular needles for two circulars technique, or one 32" or longer circular needle for Magic Loop technique, or one size smaller than size to obtain gauge, for ribbing

NOTIONS
Yarn Needle
3 Stitch Markers
Waste Yarn

GAUGE
32 sts and 40 rnds = 4" in stranded St st in the rnd, blocked.

Morgan Mitts

Notes:

These mitts are worked from the bottom up in the round. The small and large mitts use the same motif; the medium mitts use a slightly altered motif.

Work charts in the rnd, following all chart rows from right to left, reading them as RS rows.

DIRECTIONS

Body of Mitt

Rnd 1: With C5 and smaller needles, CO 46 (54, 60) sts per the Right Mitt Chart Row 1. Join in the rnd, being careful not to twist. PM for beg of rnd.

Continue working Right Mitt Chart for your size, changing to larger needles after the ribbing is complete, and PM on either side of the thumb gusset (bordered in green).

Rnd 54 (55, 57): Work Chart to the gusset sts, place gusset sts onto waste yarn, CO 1 st as charted, finish rnd.

Complete Right Mitt Chart, changing back to smaller needles for the top ribbing and BO.

Thumb

Starting at the CO stitch on the palm, working the Top of Thumb Chart for your size, PU and K3 sts as charted, place thumb gusset sts back onto needles and work, PU and K3 sts. PM for beg of rnd.

Work remainder of thumb as charted, changing to smaller needles for ribbing. BO K-wise.

Repeat for second mitt with the Left Chart for your size.

Finishing

Weave in ends, wash and block.

Legend:

- Cast on — Cast on one stitch with color shown
- knit — knit stitch
- purl — purl stitch
- No Stitch — Placeholder - No stitch made.
- Bind Off — Bind off one stitch in color shown
- make one right (MR) — Place a firm backward loop over the right needle, so that the yarn end goes towards the back
- make one left (ML) — Place a firm backward loop over the right needle, so that the yarn end goes towards the front
- k2tog — Knit two stitches together as one stitch
- p2tog — Purl two stitches together as one stitch
- ssk — Slip one stitch as if to knit, Slip another stitch as if to knit. Insert left-hand needle into front of these 2 stitches and knit them together
- Pick up and knit — Pick up one stitch and knit with color shown
- Thumb Gusset — Place markers either side

Colors: MC, C1, C2, C3, C4, C5, C6, C7

Small Top of Thumb Chart

Small Right Chart

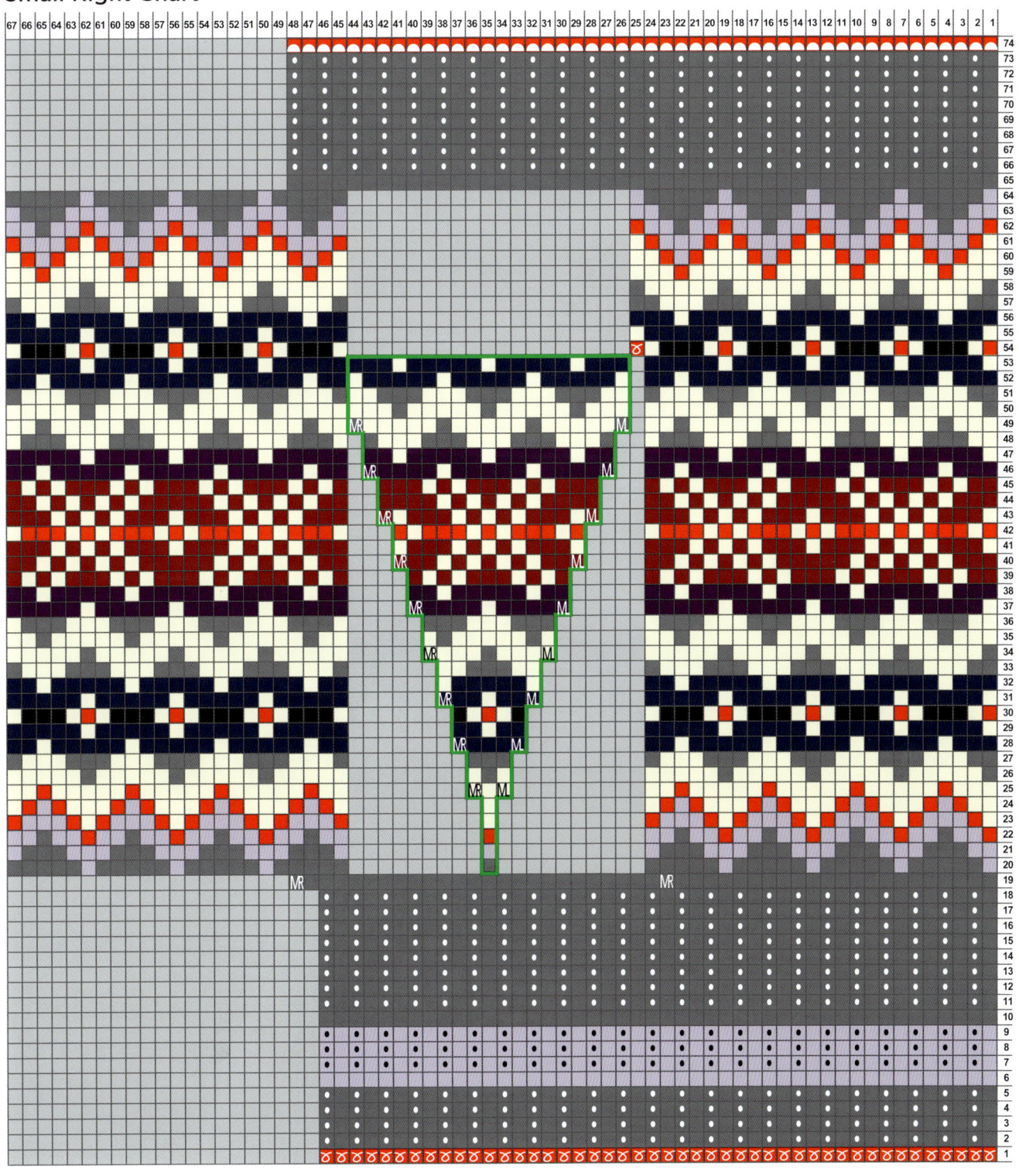

Morgan Mitts

Small Left Chart

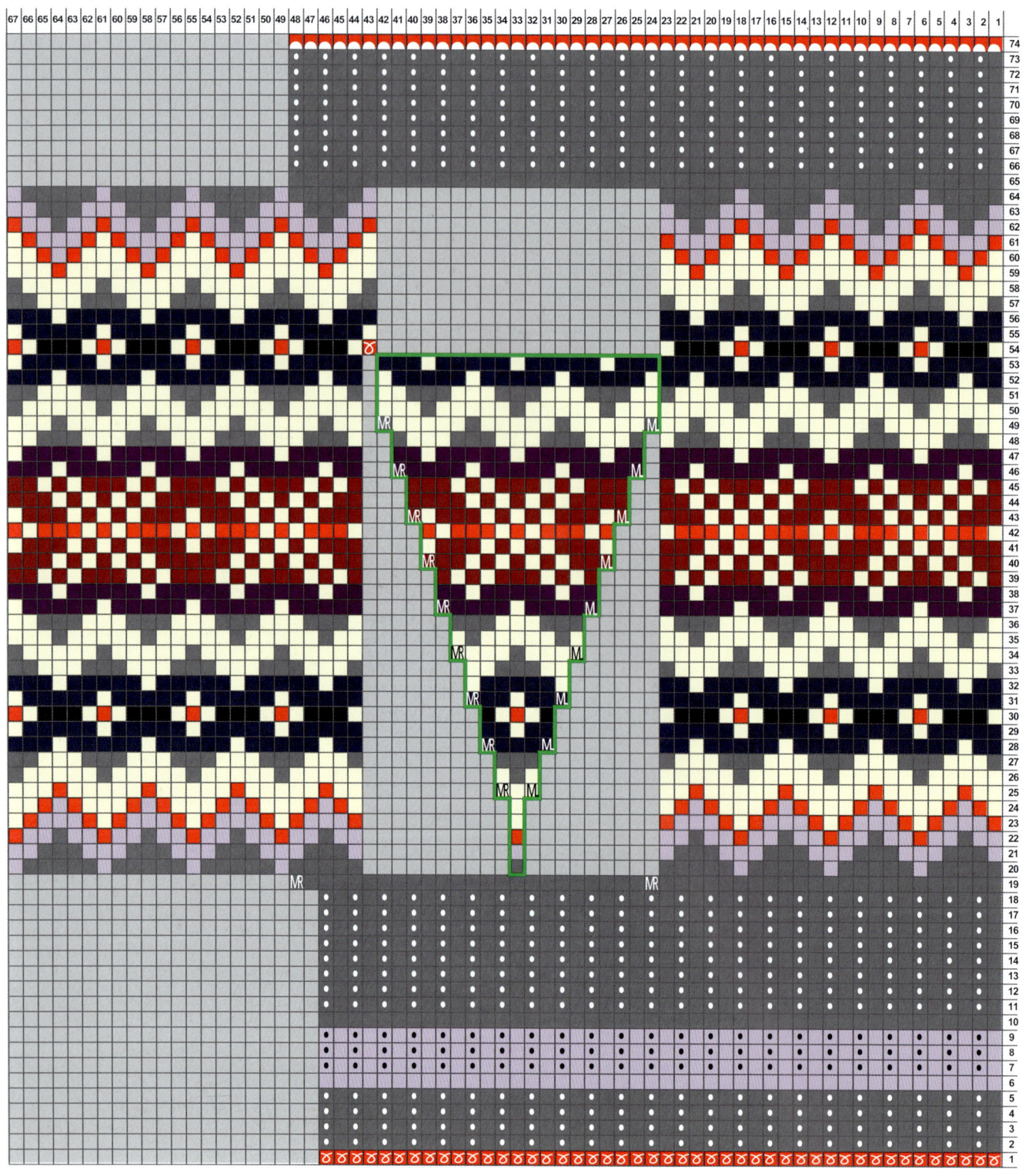

Medium Right Chart

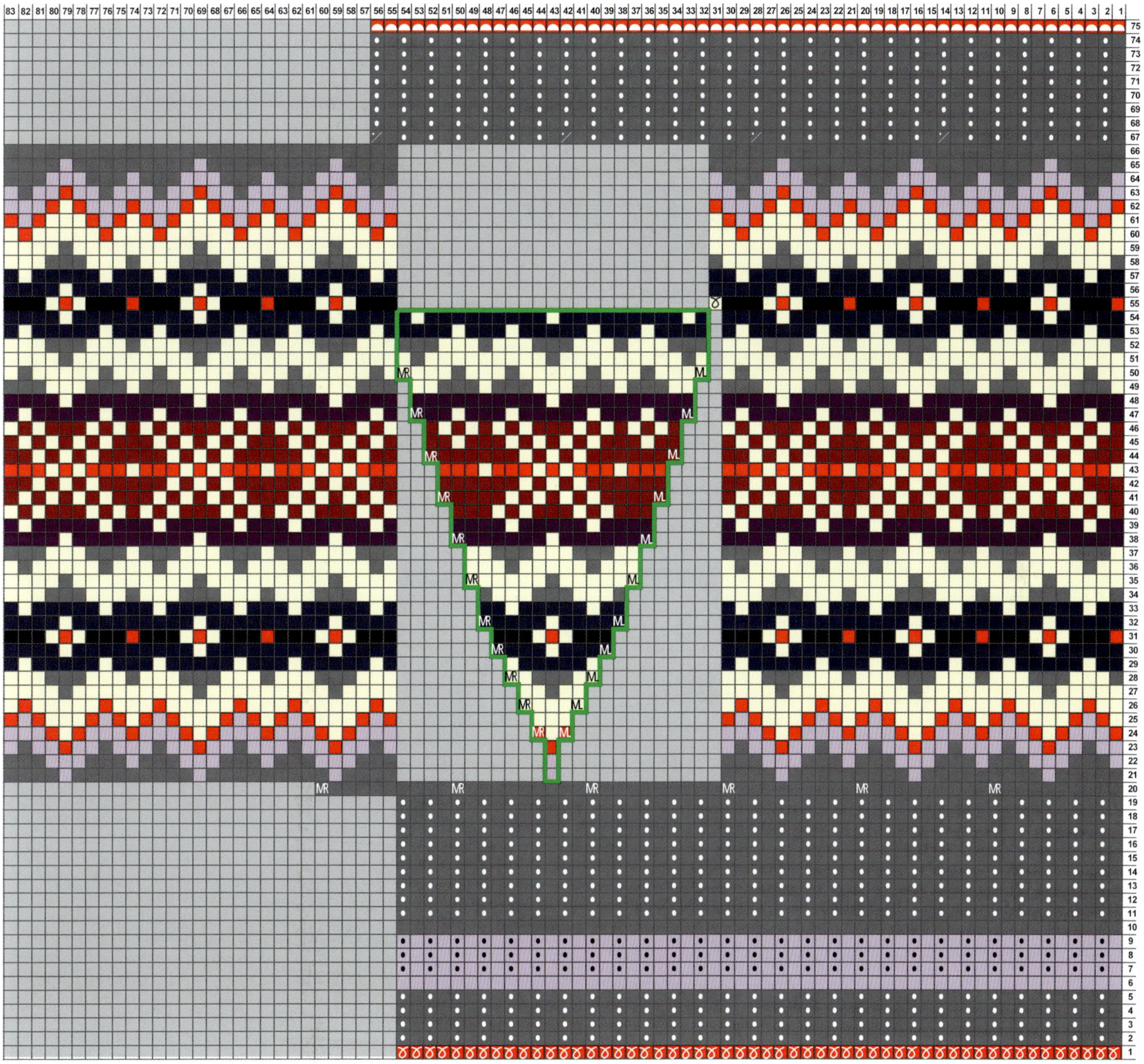

Medium Top of Thumb Chart

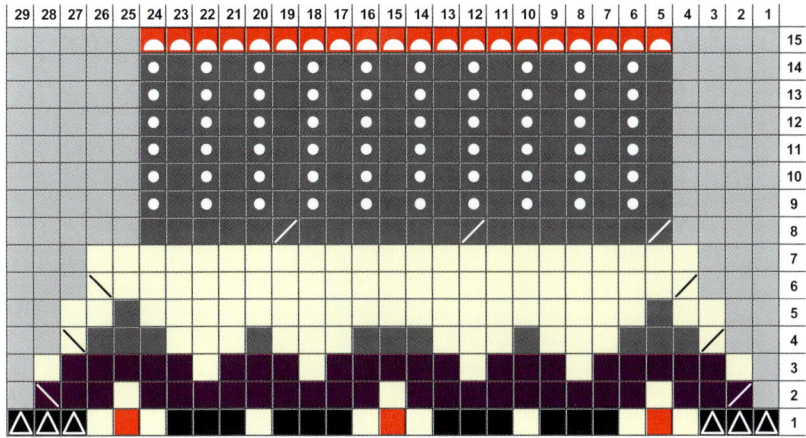

Medium Left Chart

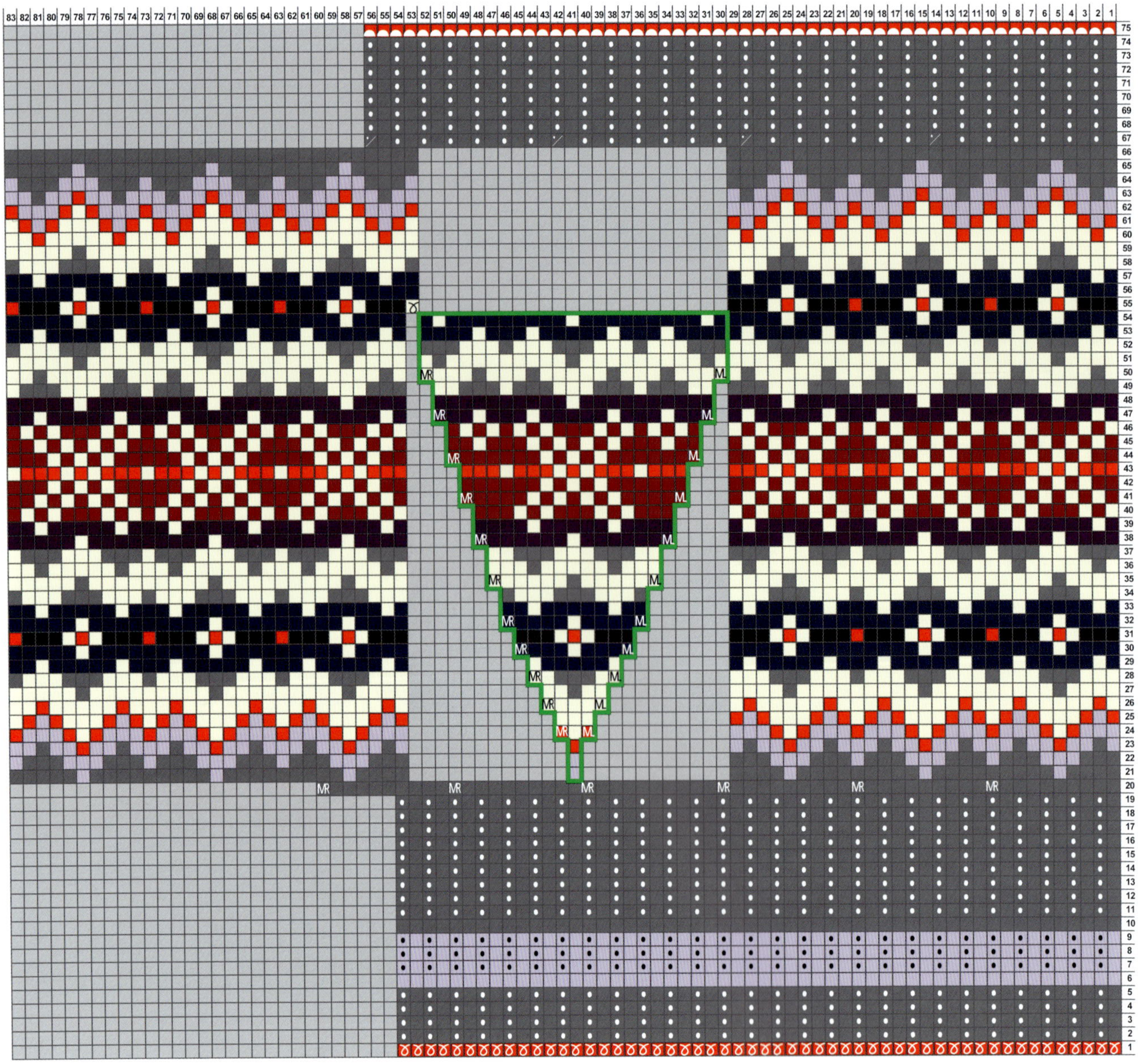

Large Top of Thumb Chart

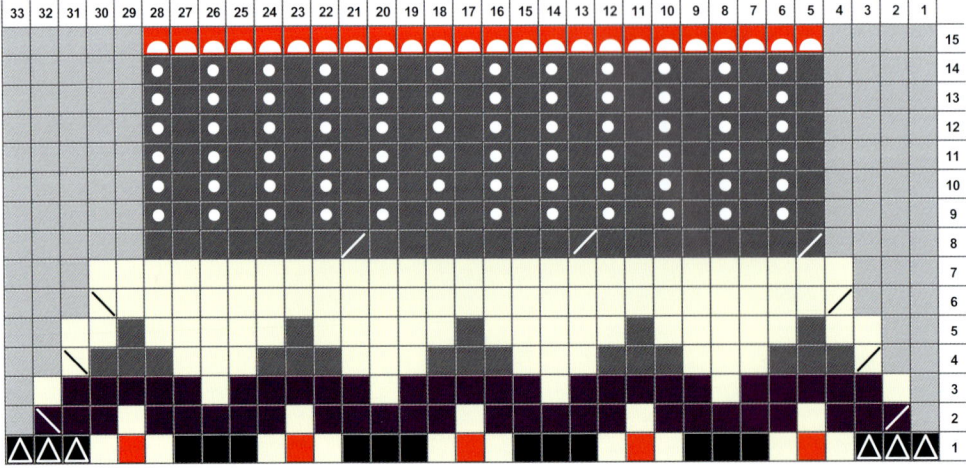

38 Morgan Mitts

Large Right Chart

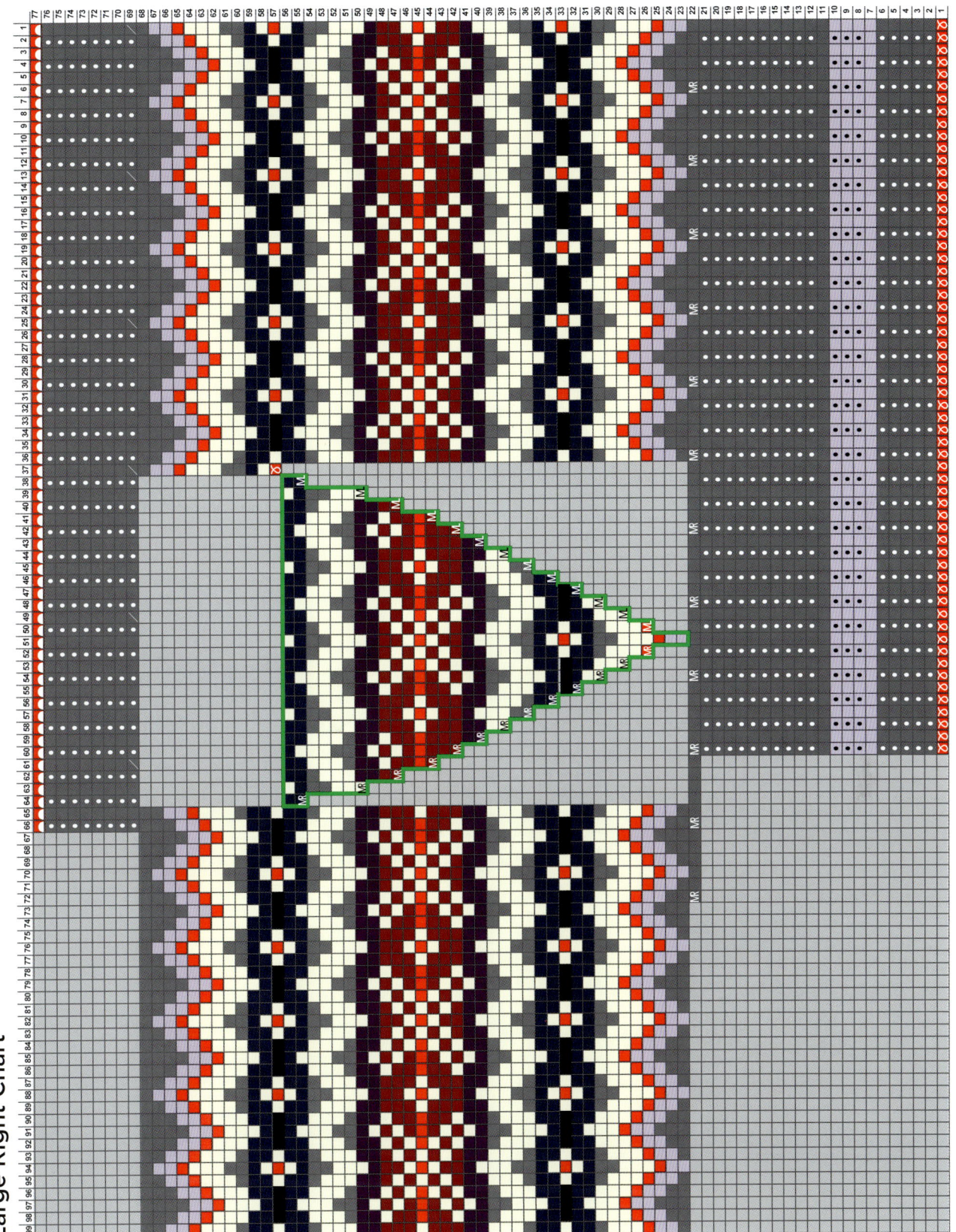

Morgan Mitts 39

Large Left Chart

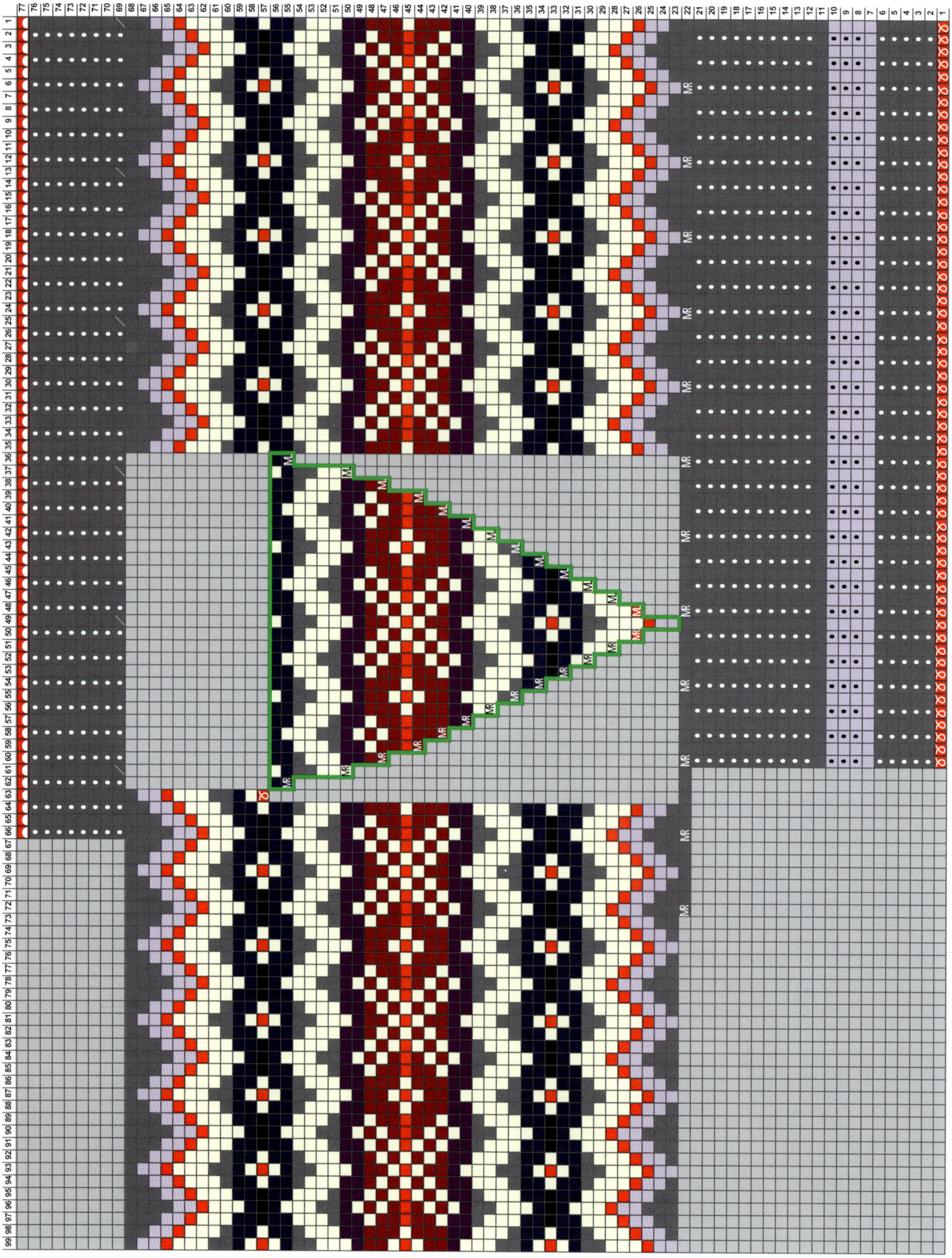

40 Morgan Mitts

FIRESIDE TABLET COVER

by Stana D. Sortor

FINISHED MEASUREMENTS
Tablet cover: 8.5" wide and 12.25" long, blocked
I-pad cover: 8" wide and 10.25" long, blocked

YARN
Knit Picks Palette (100% Peruvian Highland Wool; 231 yards/50g): MC Golden Heather 24005, C1 Cream 23730, C2 Salsa Heather 24003, C3 Garnet Heather 24015, C4 Bark 23737, 1 ball each

NEEDLES
US 3 (3.25mm) DPNs or two 24" circular needles for two circulars technique, or one 32" or longer circular needle for Magic Loop technique, or size to obtain gauge

NOTIONS
Yarn Needle
Stitch Markers
Crochet Hook and Scarp Yarn (or as preferred for Provisional CO)
Stitch holder or spare circular needle and DPNs
Button

GAUGE
28 sts and 34 rows = 4" in stranded St st in the round, blocked

Fireside Tablet Cover

Notes:

Starting with a provisional cast on, this cover is knit in the round in a Fair Isle pattern to the flap, which is then knit flat. The bottom is closed with a 3- Needle Bind off. A small I-cord loop is knit for the button closure.

Fireside Charts 1 and 2 are worked in the round from bottom to top, reading each row from right to left as RS Rnds.
Fireside Charts 3 and 4 are worked flat from bottom to top, working back and forth, all RS odd rows work from right to left, and all WS even rows work from left to right.

I-Cord (worked over 3 sts)
All Rows: K3, slide sts to other end of DPN pulling yarn firmly, do not turn.
Repeat Row until I-Cord reaches desired length.

3-Needle Bind Off
Position two needles with an equal number of sts held parallel to each other and RS of work facing together.
* With a DPN, K2tog with one st from each needle at the same time, repeat from * once more, then BO a st by passing the first st worked on the RH needle over the 2nd st worked on the RH needle. Continue in this manner until the required number of sts are bound off.

DIRECTIONS
Body:
Using the Provisional CO technique of your choice, CO 120 sts. Attach MC, being careful not to twist the sts, and begin to K in the rnd.
Rnd 1: K.
For the I-pad Cover Only: After Rnd 1 continue with Rnd 17 from the Fireside Chart 1, replacing C4 with C3 for Rnd 17 only.

Rnds 2 – 47: Work Fireside Chart 1, repeating each chart row ten times around.
Rnds 48 – 96: Work Fireside Chart 2, repeating each chart row ten times around.

Transfer the last 60 sts onto a stitch holder or extra circular needle. Starting with Row 97, the remaining 60 sts will be worked flat, using C1. Do not turn the work around.

Row 97: P.
Row 98: P.
Row 99: K.
Row 100: P.
Row 101: K.
Row 102: P.
Row 103: BO all sts.

Flap:
Transfer the last 60 sts from stitch holder to working needles, and attach C1 yarn.

Row 97: K.
Row 98: P.

Rows 99 - 126: Work Fireside Chart 3, repeating each chart row five times across.
Rows 127 - 154: Work Fireside Chart 4, repeating each chart row five times across.
Row 155: BO all sts.

Remove the scrap yarn from the provisionally CO sts and place the resulting live sts on two spare needles, with 60 sts on each needle.

Turn the work inside out and arrange so folded sides are even with the side edges of the flap. With MC, use 3-Needle Bind Off to seam the front and back together.

Button Loop
CO 3 sts in C2. Work I-cord for 2" then BO.

Finishing
Arrange the two layers of the flap together. Use safety pin to secure it. Sew the two layers together. Fold the front at Row 28 of Chart 3 (Reverse St. st row), and sew the folded layer to the inside of the cover.

Sew the I-cord loop to the middle part of the flap. Sew the button to the front of the cover.

Weave in ends, wash and block to the measurements.

Legend:

☐ **knit**
RS: knit stitch
WS: purl stitch

• **purl**
RS: purl stitch
WS: knit stitch

☐ MC
☐ C1
☐ C2
☐ C3
☐ C4

Charts 1&2 are worked in the round, while charts 3&4 are back and forth.

Chart 1

Chart 2

Chart 3

Chart 4

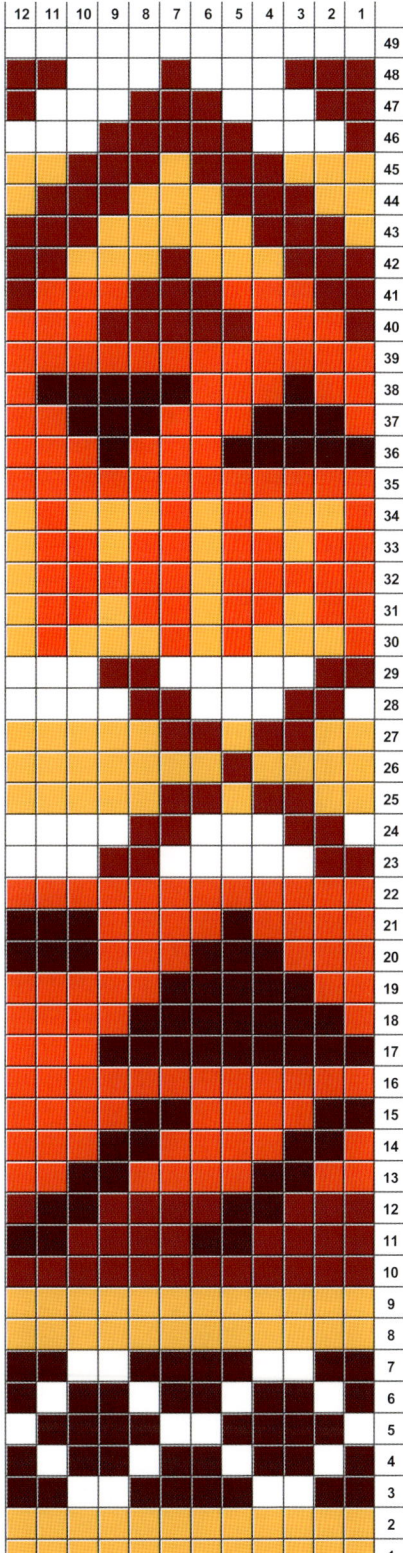
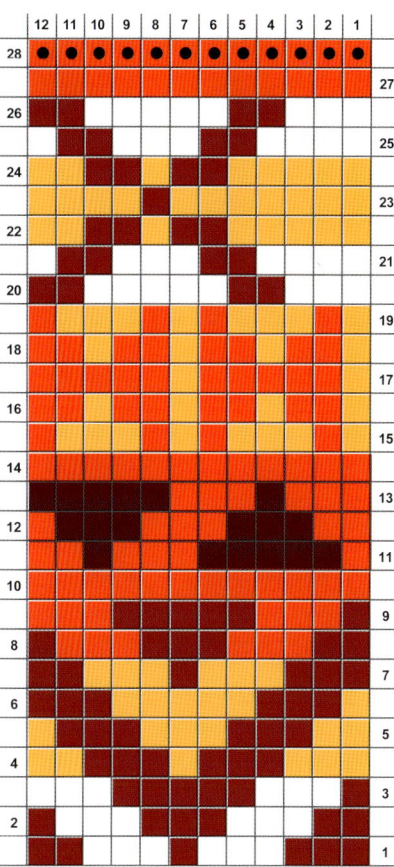
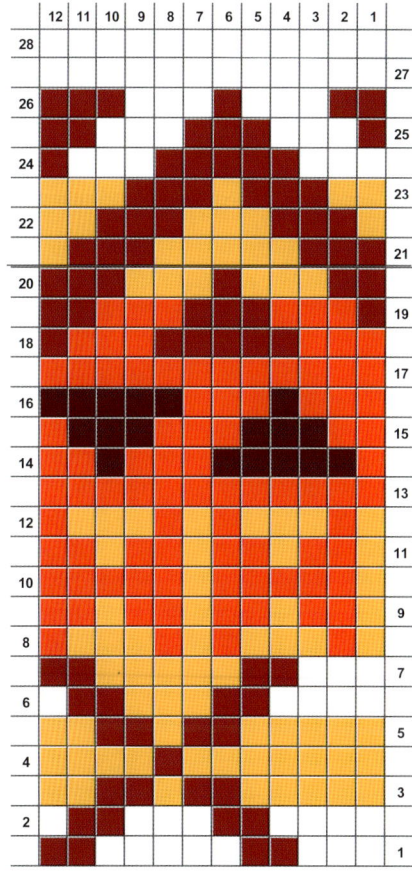

Fireside Tablet Cover   45

SHEA COWL

by Abbyeknits

FINISHED MEASUREMENTS
25" circumference x 15" tall; one size fits all

YARN
Knit Picks Swish Worsted (100% Superwash Merino Wool;110 yards/50g): C1 Lemongrass Heather 24093, 1 ball, C2 Marble Heather 25153, 2 balls, C3 Indigo Heather 24097, 1 ball, C4 Honey 26066, 1 ball, C5 Hollyberry 25148, 1 ball

NEEDLES
US 10 (6mm) DPNs or 16" circular needle, or size to obtain gauge

NOTIONS
Yarn Needle

GAUGE
16 sts and 20 rnds = 4" in stranded St st in the rnd, blocked

Shea Cowl

Notes:
This cowl is worked in the round, featuring increases after the first border, and decreases before the finishing border.
Follow all chart rows from right to left, reading them as RS rows.

DIRECTIONS

Start Border
With C1, CO 90sts and join in the rnd, being careful not to twist sts. PM to mark beginning of rnd.
Rnds 1, 3 & 5: K.
Rnds 2 & 4: P.
Rnd 6: *P8, PFB; rep *to end of rnd. 100 sts.

Body
Work Chart Rnds 1-32, repeating 10 times around. Repeat Rnds 1-32 once more, for a total of 64 rnds.

End Border
Rnd 1: With C1 *K8, K2tog; rep from * to end of rnd. 90 sts.
Rnds 2, 4 & 6: P.
Rnds 3 & 5: K.
BO.

Finishing
Weave in ends, wash and block to finished measurements.

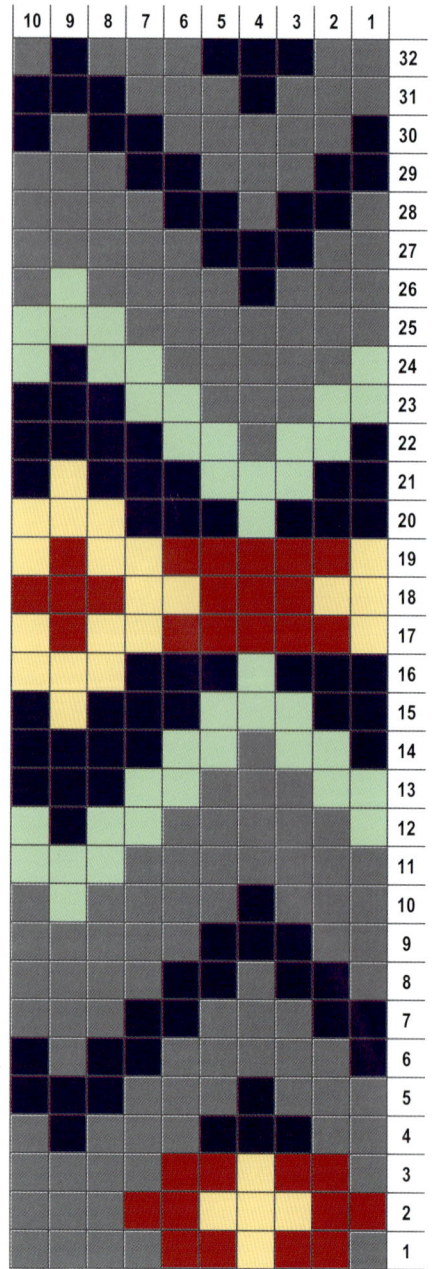

SNOW DAY TEA COZY

by Emily Kintigh

FINISHED MEASUREMENTS
11.25" circumference x 5.75" tall without loop, to fit a 2 cup globe tea pot

YARN
Knit Picks Wool of the Andes Worsted (100% Peruvian Highland Wool; 110 yards/50g): MC Solstice Heather 25066, C1 Fjord Heather 25647, C2 White 24065, 1 ball each

NEEDLES
US 6 (4mm) circular needles and DPNs, or size to obtain gauge US 4 (3.5mm) straight or circular needles, or two sizes below gauge needle

NOTIONS
Yarn Needle
Stitch Markers
Size D Crochet hook
One .75" white button

GAUGE
22 sts and 28 rows = 4" in St st on larger needles, blocked

Snow Day Tea Cozy

Notes:
The hem at the bottom is worked flat, the work is then joined in the round (adding steeks) and the rest of the tea cozy is worked in the round.

Steeks are used to form the holes for the spout and handle of the teapot. The seven stitch sections CO after working the hem are the steek stitches. The charts include directions for working these stitches to form vertical striped steeks.

A tutorial on preparing and cutting steeks can be found here: http://tutorials.knitpicks.com/how-to-prepare-cut-a-steek/

When working charts in the rnd, follow all chart rows from right to left, reading them as RS rows.

DIRECTIONS

Hem
With MC and smaller needles, CO 62 sts.
Row 1: (K2, P2) to last 2 sts, K2.
Row 2: (P2, K2) to last 2 sts, P2.
Rep Rows 1-2 two more times.

Main Body
Switch to larger needles and C2.
Row 1: K31, CO 7 sts, PM, K31, CO 7 sts. 76 sts.
Next Rnd: PM and join in the rnd. K to end.

Work Snow Day Chart between the beginning of the rnd and the marker, then again between the marker and the end of the rnd. Note: The pattern repeat of Sts 1-8 is worked three times before moving on to Sts 9-22 of the Snow Day Chart. The last seven sts of the chart are the steek.

Next Rnd: With C2, K31, BO 7 sts, remove M, K to end. 69 sts.
Next Rnd: K62 sts, PM, K to end.

Top
Work Rnds 1-2 of Border Chart repeating Sts 1-2 to M and working Sts 3-9 from M to end. Work Rnd 3 of Border Chart to M, remove M, BO 7 sts. 62 sts.

Next Rnd: With C2, K to end, CO 2 sts. 64 sts.
Next Rnd: (SSK, K28, K2tog) to end. 60 sts.

Work Top Decreases Chart, repeating six times across rnd. 6 sts.

Next Rnd: K2tog to end. 3 sts.
Transfer sts to single DPN. Work in I-Cord for 3". BO all sts. Sew end of I-Cord to beginning of I-Cord to form a loop.

Button Loop
With MC and crochet hook, make a 1.5" chain. Sew both ends of chain to one side of the hem to form a loop. Sew the button to the other side of the hem.

Finishing
Use crochet hook to reinforce along the middle of the steeks. Cut steeks, fold in and secure to inside of tea cozy. Weave in ends, wash and block.

Snow Day

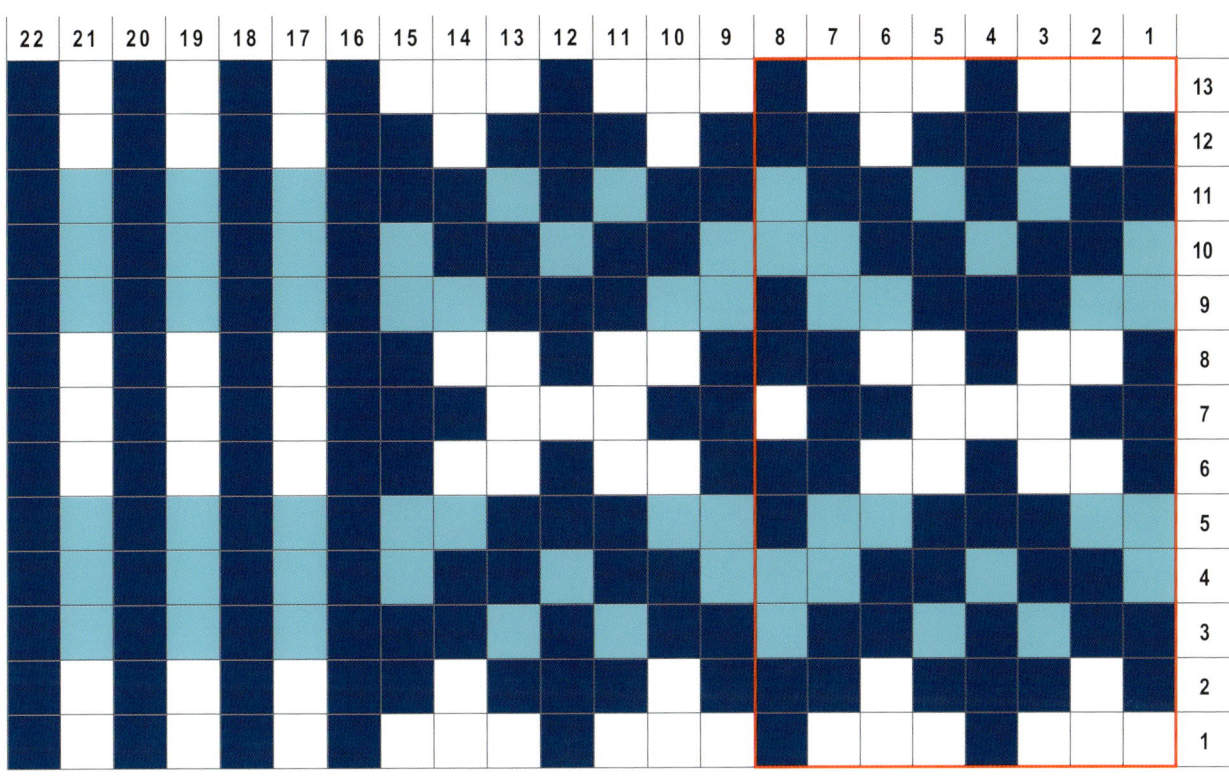

Top Decrease

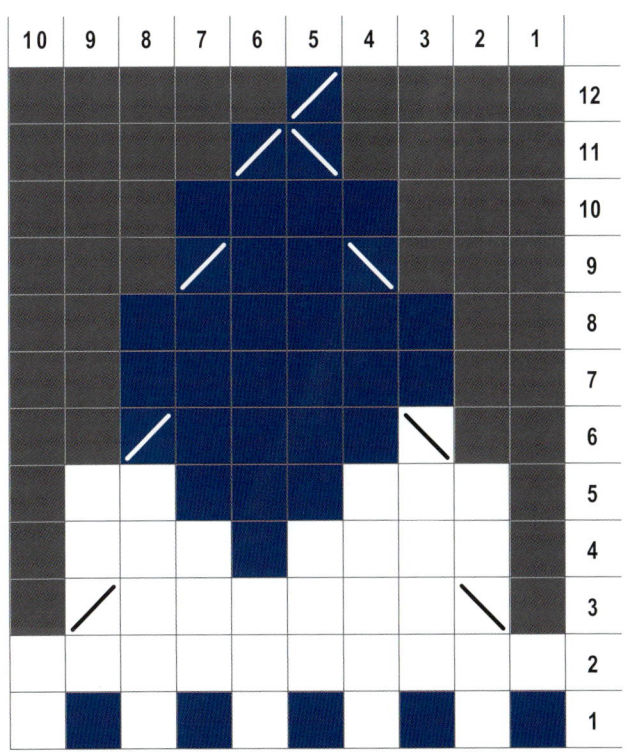

Legend:

- knit — knit stitch
- ssk — in indicated color
- k2tog — in indicated color
- no stitch
- MC
- C1
- C2
- Pattern Repeat

Border

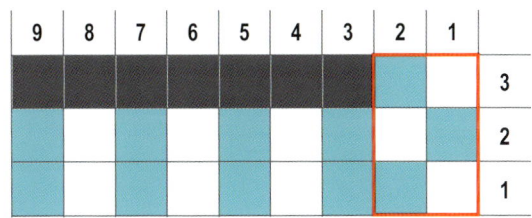

Snow Day Tea Cozy 53

TO THE TOP HAT

by Gabrielle Vézina

FINISHED MEASUREMENTS
Sizes: Newborn (Baby, Toddler, Child, Adult S, Adult L) 12 (14, 16, 17.5, 20.5, 23.25)" circumference at brim to fit head circumference 13 (15, 17, 18.5, 21.5, 24.25)"

YARN
Knit Picks Swish DK (100% Superwash Merino Wool; 123 yards/50g): MC Cobblestone Heather 24313 1 (1, 1, 1, 1, 2) balls, C1 White 24064 1 ball, C2 Honey 26061 1 ball

Alternate 2 color version:
Knit Picks Swish DK (100% Superwash Merino Wool; 123 yards/50g): MC Cobblestone Heather 24313 1 (1, 1, 1, 1, 2) balls, C1 White 24064 1 ball

NEEDLES
US 5 (3.75mm) DPNs or two 24" circular needles for two circulars technique, or one 32" or longer circular needle for Magic Loop technique, or size to obtain gauge
US 2 (2.75mm) DPNs or two 24" circular needles for two circulars technique, or one 32" or longer circular needle for Magic Loop technique, or size to obtain gauge

NOTIONS
Yarn Needle
1 Stitch Marker

GAUGE
18 sts and 20 rnds = 4" in stranded St st in the rnd on larger needle, blocked
22 sts and 24 rnds = 4" in 1x1 Ribbing in the rnd on smaller needle, blocked

For pattern support, contact hello@gabriellevezina.com

To the Top Hat

Notes:
This hat is worked from the bottom to the top, with a ribbing section at the bottom followed with a Fair Isle pattern made of two colors. The top of the hat is made with a third color to add some brightness to the long days of winter. Alternatively, the top can be made with just the C1 color.

When working charts in the rnd, follow all chart rows from right to left, reading them as RS rows.

1x1 Ribbing (worked in the rnd over an even number of sts)
All Rnds: (K1, P1) around.
Repeat for pattern.

DIRECTIONS

With smaller needles and MC, CO 64 (76, 88, 96, 112, 128) sts. PM, join to work in the rnd being careful not to twist sts.

Brim
K for 4 (4, 4, 6, 6, 6) rnds.
Work in 1x1 Ribbing for 4 (6, 8, 10, 12, 12) rnds.

Switch to larger needles and join C1.

With MC and C1, work Chart 1 (1, 1, 1, 2, 2) over all sts, ending with Rnd 23 (23, 23, 23, 39, 47).
Cut MC. For the 3-color version, cut C1 and join C2.

K for 0 (1, 4, 8, 6, 4) rnds.

Baby Size only: (K17, K2tog) around. 4 sts dec. 72 sts.

Crown
Rnd 1: (K6, K2tog) around. 56 (63, 77, 84, 98, 112) sts.
Rnd 2: K all sts.
Rnd 3: (K5, K2tog) around. 48 (54, 66, 72, 84, 96) sts.
Rnd 4: K all sts.
Rnd 5: (K4, K2tog) around. 40 (45, 55, 60, 70, 80) sts.
Rnd 6: (K3, K2tog) around. 32 (36, 44, 48, 56, 64) sts.
Rnd 7: (K2, K2tog) around. 24 (27, 33, 36, 42, 48) sts.
Rnd 8: (K1, K2tog) around. 16 (18, 22, 24, 28, 32) sts.
Rnd 9: K2tog around. 8 (9, 11, 12, 14, 16) sts.
Rnd 10: K2tog around until last 0 (1, 1, 0, 0, 0) st, K 0 (1, 1, 0, 0, 0). 4 (5, 6, 6, 7, 8) sts.

Cut yarn, thread through remaining sts.

Finishing
Weave in ends, wash and block to desired measurements.

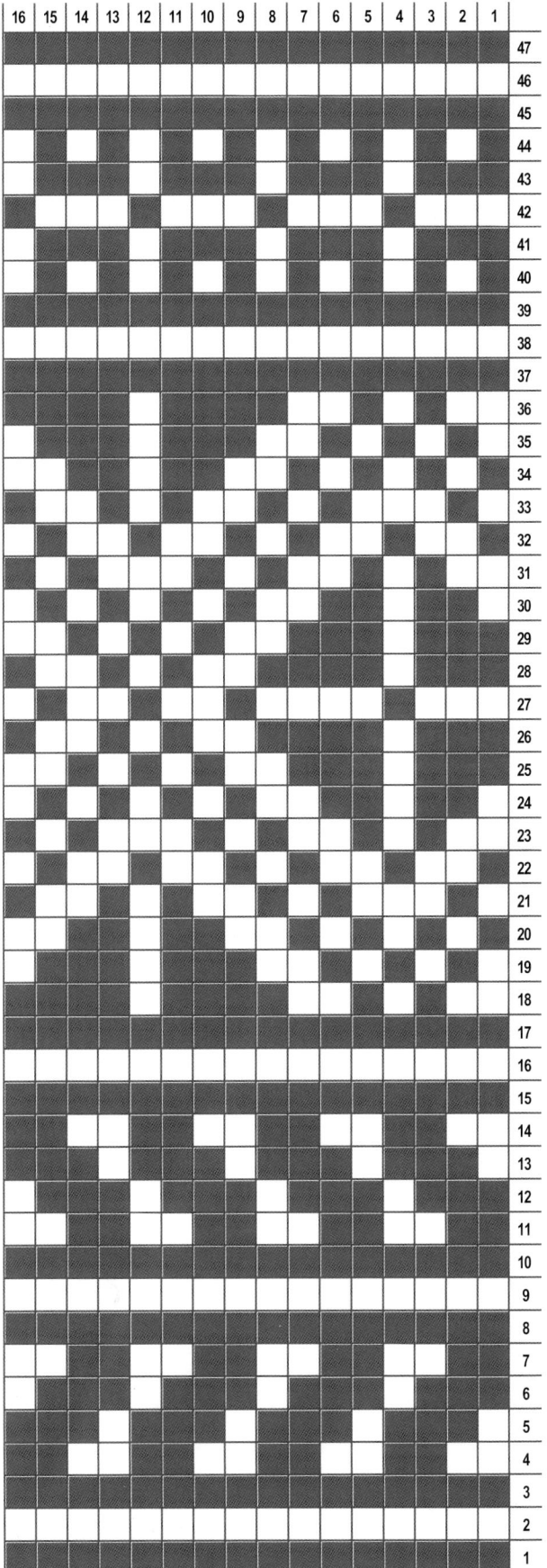

To the Top Hat 57

BLODWEN COWL

by Stephannie Tallent

FINISHED MEASUREMENTS
22.5" circumference x 8.75" tall

YARN
Knit Picks Palette (100% Peruvian Highland Wool; 231 yards/50g):
MC Finnley Heather 26043, C1 Turmeric 24251, C2 Serrano 24553, C3 Garnet Heather 24015, C4 Marble Heather 24244, C5 Asphalt Heather 24243, C6 Black 23729, C7 Cornmeal 24252, 1 ball each

NEEDLES
US 2 (3mm) DPNs or two 24" circular needles for two circulars technique, or one 32" or longer circular needle for Magic Loop technique, or size to obtain gauge
US 1 (2.5mm) DPNs or two 24" circular needles for two circulars technique, or one 32" or longer circular needle for Magic Loop technique, or one size smaller than size to obtain gauge

NOTIONS
Yarn Needle
Stitch Markers

GAUGE
32 sts and 33 rows = 4" in stranded St st in the rnd, blocked

Blodwen Cowl

Notes:
This cowl is worked in the round from the bottom up, with the colorwork repeat charted. You can easily alter the circumference by working more or fewer repeats of the 30-stitch chart, or alter the height by working additional repeats of Rnds 1-30 before finishing with Rnds 31-52.

Work charts in the rnd, follow all chart rows from right to left, reading them as RS rows.

Ribbing (in the rnd over an even number of sts)
Rnd 1: *K1, P1; rep from * to end.

DIRECTIONS

Lower Ribbing
CO 180 sts with C1 and smaller needles and join in the rnd, being careful not to twist sts. PM for beg of rnd.

Work Ribbing for 10 rounds.

Body
Change to larger needles. Work Chart 6 times to end of rnd. Complete Rnds 1-52 once.

Upper Ribbing
Change to smaller needles. With C1, work Ribbing for 10 rnds. BO in pattern.

Finishing
Weave in ends, wash and block.

Blodwen Cowl Chart

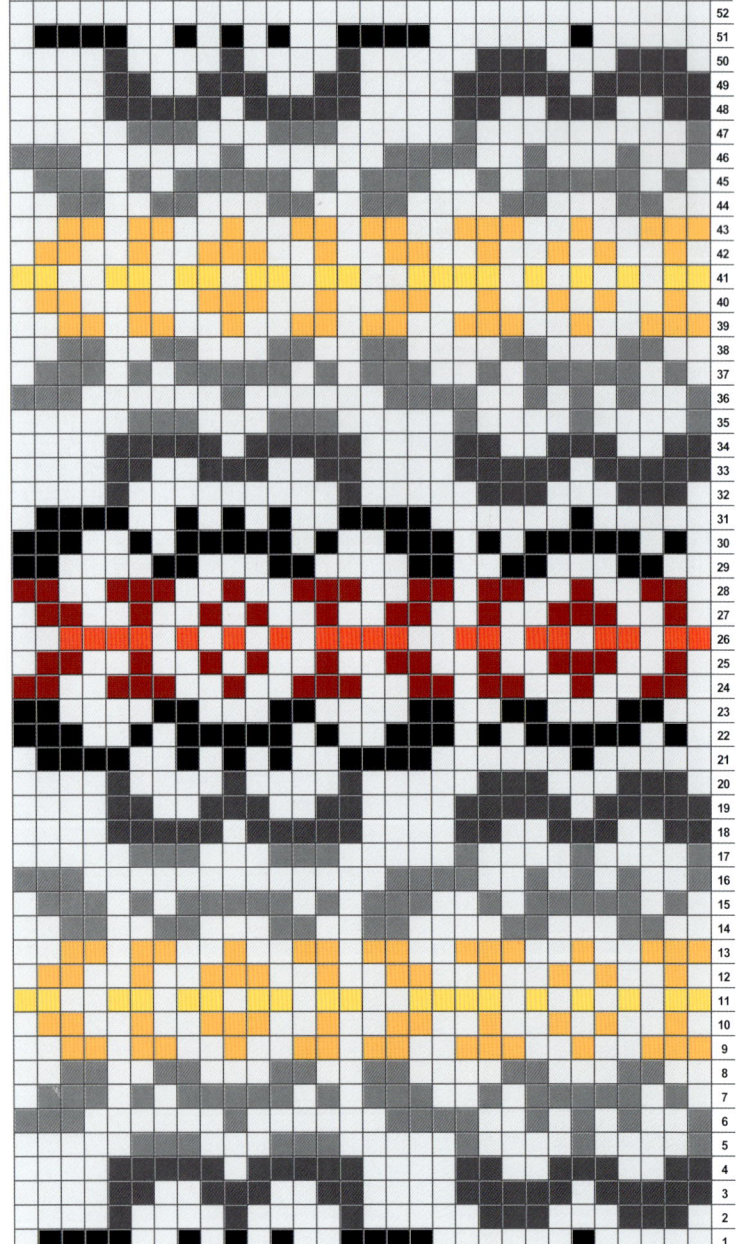

Legend:
- knit / knit stitch
- MC
- C1
- C2
- C3
- C4
- C5
- C6
- C7

CATALINA HOT WATER BOTTLE COVER

by Kendra Nitta

FINISHED MEASUREMENTS
Approximately 6.5" wide x 7.75" high (to bottom of spout ribbing), blocked. To fit 1L hot water bottle

YARN
Knit Picks Palette (100% Peruvian Highland Wool; 231 yards/50g): C1 Cream 23730, C2 Semolina 24250, C3 Turmeric 24251, C4 Silver 24586, C5 Mist 23733, C6 Ash 23731, 1 ball each

NEEDLES
US 2.5 (3mm) 12" and 24" circular needles, or two 24" circular needles for two circulars technique, or size to obtain gauge

NOTIONS
Yarn Needle

GAUGE
26 sts and 36 rnds = 4" in stranded St st in the round, blocked

Catalina Hot Water Bottle Cover

Notes:
Combining traditional designs in a modern palette makes this hot water bottle cover both cozy and fresh. Working in the round, the piece knits up quickly with no seaming and almost no finishing. It's a great project for learning to read a color chart and practicing stranded knitting. It's also a chance to practice the ribbed version of Jeny's Surprisingly Stretchy Bind-off.

The pattern is written for a small 1 liter hot water bottle. For a 2 liter large hot water bottle (approximately 7.5" wide), choose a DK weight yarn such as Swish DK and work at a gauge of approximately 22 sts and 28 rows = 4".

Work the chart in the rnd, following all chart rows from right to left, reading them as RS rows.

K2, P2 Rib (worked in the rnd over multiple of 4 sts)
All Rnds: K2, P2 to end.

Judy's Magic Cast-on (JMCO)
Instructions for JMCO can be found at http://tutorials.knitpicks.com/judys-magic-cast-on/

DIRECTIONS
This pattern uses two circular needles to CO and work the first 3 rnds. You can then continue to work on two circular needles, which will make it easy to try the piece on your hot water bottle as you go, or transfer the sts from Needle 2 to a 12-inch circular needle. You will use two circular needles again to shape the top.

Body
Using JMCO and C2, CO 36 sts on each circular needle; 72 sts total.

Inc Rnd: On Needle 1, KFB, K to last 2 sts, KFB, K1; rep for Needle 2. 38 sts on each circular needle; 76 sts total.
Rep Inc Rnd twice more. 42 sts on each circular needle; 84 sts total.
Transfer sts to one 12-inch circular needle, if desired.
Work 4 rnds even.

Fair Isle Motif
Work Rows 1-57 of Chart in stranded St st. Note: Each row is worked twice per round.

Shape Top
Work 3 rnds even with C2 only. If needed, transfer last 42 sts to Needle 2.

Dec Rnd: On Needle 1, K1, K2tog, K to last 3 sts, SSK, K1; rep for Needle 2. 40 sts on each circular needle; 80 sts total.
Rep Dec Rnd twice more. 36 sts on each circular needle; 72 sts total.

Spout Ribbing
Work in K2, P2 Rib for 5" or desired length. Work Jeny's Surprisingly Stretchy Bind-Off in K2, P2 rib as follows, or use other very stretchy BO:

BO Setup: K1, wrap the yarn around the right-hand needle in a reverse YO, from back to front; K1, pass first K st and YO over the K st.
BO Step 1: Wrap the yarn around the right-hand needle in a YO, from front to back; P1; pass K st and YO over the P st.
BO Step 2: Wrap the yarn around the right-hand needle in a YO, from front to back; P1; pass P st and YO over the P st.
BO Step 3: Wrap the yarn around the right-hand needle in a reverse YO, from back to front; K1; pass P st over YO and K st.
BO Step 4: Wrap the yarn around the right-hand needle in a reverse YO, from back to front; K1; pass K st over YO and K st.
Rep BO Steps 1-4 until 1 st remains.

Cut the yarn and pull it through the last st.

Finishing
Weave in ends, wash and block to finished measurements.

Catalina Hot Water Bottle Cover Chart

Legend:

 knit — knit stitch

 C1

 C2

 C3

 C4

 C5

C6

SHAELA COWL

by Courtney Spainhower

FINISHED MEASUREMENTS
14.75" tall x 19.5" circumference, blocked

YARN
Knit Picks Palette (100% Peruvian Highland Wool; 231 yards/50g):
MC Cream 23730, C1 Silver 24586, C2 Asphalt Heather 24243, 1 ball each

NEEDLES
US 3 (3.25mm) 16" circular needles, or size to obtain gauge

NOTIONS
Yarn Needle
Stitch Markers
Spare Needles or scrap yarn

GAUGE
32 sts and 32 rnds = 4" in stranded St st in the rnd, blocked.

Shaela Cowl

Notes:
Cowl is worked starting with two pieces worked flat, then joined and worked in rounds from the bottom up. The stranded color work sections are fully charted. Be careful to allow plenty of room for yarn floats so that the fabric doesn't become too tight.

1x2 Rib (worked flat over multiple of 3 sts plus 2)
Row 1 (RS): K1, (K1, P1, K1) to last st, K1.
Row 2 (WS): K1, (P1, K1, P1) to last st, K1.

1x1 Rib (in the round over an even number of sts)
Every Rnd: (K1, P1) to end.

DIRECTIONS
Cowl
The cowl is worked flat from the bottom up starting with a split hem, then joined and worked in the round.

Front Hem
With MC, loosely CO 77 sts.
Work 1x2 Rib repeating Rows 1 and 2 twelve times.
Break yarn and place sts onto spare needles or scrap yarn.

Back Hem
Work as for Front Hem, but do not break yarn.
With RS facing, PM, CO1 st, K across Front Hem, CO1 st, K across Back Hem, and join to work in the rnd – 156 sts.

Body
P 1 rnd.
K 2 rnds.
Work Rnds 1-31 of Chart 1.
With C2, K75, K2tog, K to last 2 sts, K2tog. 2 sts dec. 154 sts.
Work Rnds 1-30 of Chart 2.
With C2, K76, M1, K to end, M1. 2 sts inc. 156 sts.
Work Rnds 1-12 of Chart 3.
With MC, K 1 rnd.
Work 1x1 Rib for 14 rnds.
BO loosely in pattern.

Finishing
Weave in ends, wash and block to measurements.

Chart 3

Legend:
- knit / knit stitch
- MC
- C1
- C2
- Pattern Repeat

Chart 1

Chart 2

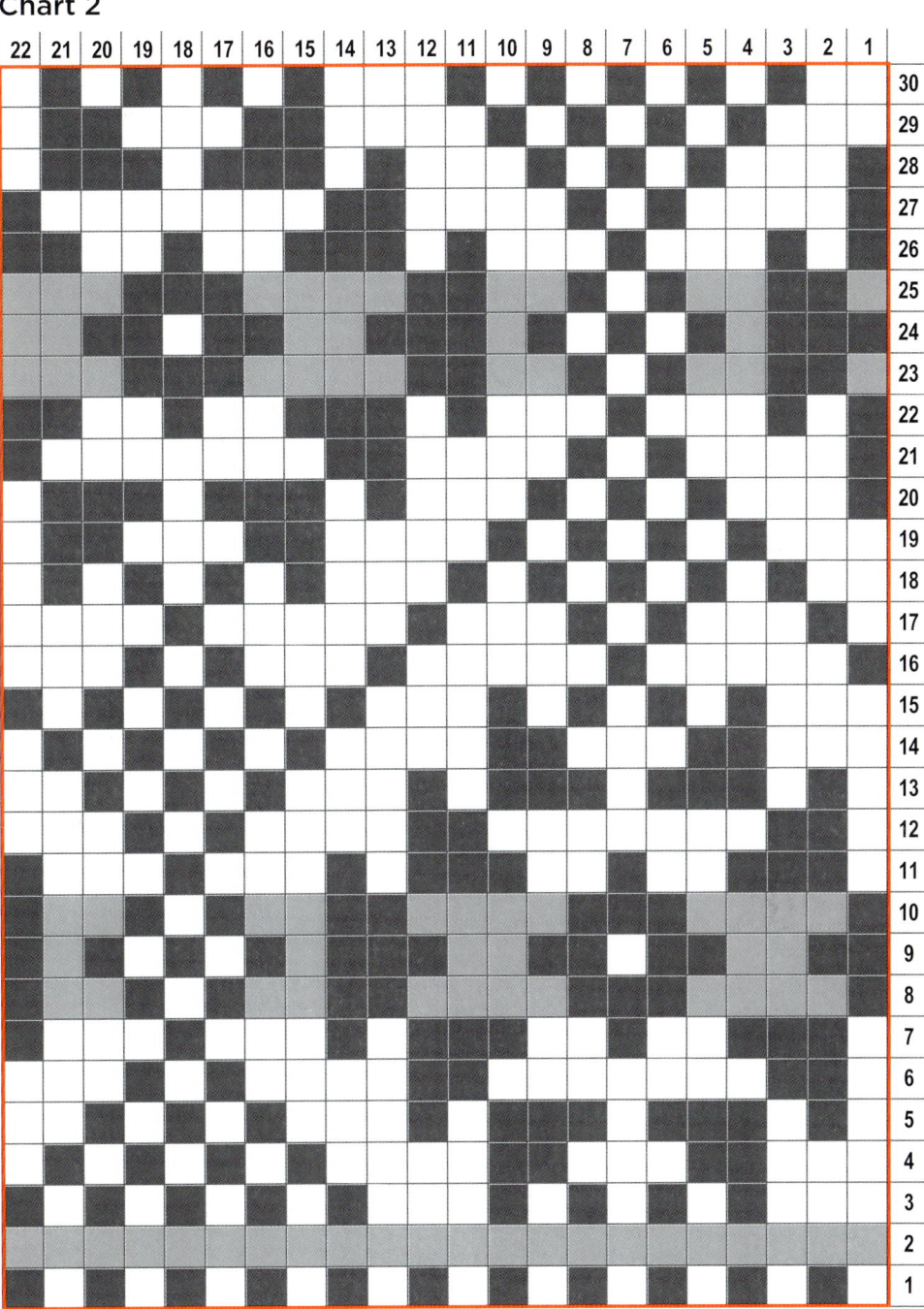

Shaela Cowl

Abbreviations							
BO	bind off	M	marker		stitch	TBL	through back loop
cn	cable needle	M1	make one stitch	RH	right hand	TFL	through front loop
CC	contrast color	M1L	make one left-leaning stitch	rnd(s)	round(s)	tog	together
CDD	Centered double dec	M1R	make one right-leaning stitch	RS	right side	W&T	wrap & turn (see specific instructions in pattern)
CO	cast on			Sk	skip		
cont	continue	MC	main color	Sk2p	sl 1, k2tog, pass slipped stitch over k2tog: 2 sts dec	WE	work even
dec	decrease(es)	P	purl			WS	wrong side
DPN(s)	double pointed needle(s)	P2tog	purl 2 sts together	SKP	sl, k, psso: 1 st dec	WYIB	with yarn in back
		PM	place marker	SL	slip	WYIF	with yarn in front
EOR	every other row	PFB	purl into the front and back of stitch	SM	slip marker	YO	yarn over
inc	increase			SSK	sl, sl, k these 2 sts tog		
K	knit	PSSO	pass slipped stitch over	SSP	sl, sl, p these 2 sts tog tbl		
K2tog	knit two sts together						
KFB	knit into the front and back of stitch	PU	pick up	SSSK	sl, sl, sl, k these 3 sts tog		
		P-wise	purlwise				
K-wise	knitwise	rep	repeat	St st	stockinette stitch		
LH	left hand	Rev St st	reverse stockinette	sts	stitch(es)		

Knit Picks yarn is both luxe and affordable—a seeming contradiction trounced! But it's not just about the pretty colors; we also care deeply about fiber quality and fair labor practices, leaving you with a gorgeously reliable product you'll turn to time and time again.

THIS COLLECTION FEATURES

Palette
Fingering Weight
100% Peruvian Highland Wool

Swish DK
DK Weight
100% Superwash Merino Wool

Swish Worsted
Worsted Weight
100% Superwash Merino Wool

Wool of the Andes Sport
Sport Weight
100% Peruvian Highland Wool

Wool of the Andes Worsted
Worsted Weight
100% Peruvian Highland Wool

View these beautiful yarns and more at www.KnitPicks.com